Reflections of Aphek

★★★★★

The Spot

Rick Watson

High Plains Creole Press
Coyote LoFI Productions
© 2013 Rick Watson

Cover art by Bill Harbort. Used by permission.

Cover design by Dustin Hansen
platypusman.com

ISBN 978-0-9899677-1-6

*

A note about this book: a saintly man, large in body and soul, in a summer of my madness, read this and took on the job of editor—he is a fine writer of novels and short stories that you should all read. He is twisted and real in a holy way, and his stories are little sweet, bitter, sacred guide books to survival on this planet—he has made it possible for me to finish this story, which was once three until it saw that it was one—He found connections where Aristotle would have run shrieking —he proofed, and waited—if you like this story and can read it as a series of long poems, he is the one to bless—it you find it as Impeni-terrible as David Foster Wallace in Infinite Jest, the fault is mine. If you sense that I am a North Dakota cross between James Joyce, St Paul and Bob Dylan, the fault will be all his and mine. Someday I will read this book again. Thank you Paul, for your soulful kindness, and remember, as Doc and Purvis know, the rotten flesh of a ghost smells good!!!

Contents:

Introduction: as good a day to die as any

To: Crazy Horse Magazine
From: Rick Watkins
Re: The Ghost of Tom Mac Wrath

Have the last issue and read it
—You missed the revolution—
North Dakota is {STILL} everywhere—[1]
Let me know if you have particular subject interests
In the area of poetry submissions that imagine
A world not so brittle and lost,
Where the conflict is worth it
And class is not glass linguistics.
Which formats do you prefer?
Can these bones breath poems to make
Art of the lost manifestos?
More poetry/with the sounds of drums
What is left to say? "E" everything, now
That is, Ego and id, the truth got lost on the way out
Of Ellis Island now that the White House sleeps behind

---

[1] says Tom McGrath

Digital walls and the statue across the street
In the park has turned itself to face the West-

***

Between Finite and Infinite, part I

"At this hour I remember everything and everyone,
Vigorously, sunkenly in
The regions that—sound and feather—
Striking a little, exist
Beyond the earth, but on the earth. Today
A new winter begins." Madrid (1937)—Pablo Neruda

What if God is not a "What"?
Or "Who", but
An "IS", and "Am"?
Then what or who
"IS"
Not about what God does or do
The who?
Who IS
Is seen in "…How…"

So if we always worry,
And the Who mates with Why
This Is, and How, then How
Is hard to find,
And we are lost
In the cannot find
And miss out on what is—BE:
Then we say,
There is no God.
God doesn't answer prayers.

2

When you're dead you're dead.
The hicks in this town
Would worship a dried up stump.

***

Some absolute Still Point—
No leaves on the Chinese Elms—
White to yellow grass—chewed short.
Only the sprigs of Creeping Juniper
And Scots pines say "green".
Spring left over at the end of summer—
The sky acts blessed to be
A perfect white sky,
But then in some spots
It goes yellow and mirrors the grass.
That shadow, I told you before,
Rises out of the east sides of the valley
And up from the earth itself,
Just after All Saints Day,
Just before Veterans Day
Or any other day.
Late afternoon
Sleeps late this autumn.
The silence at the end of the day
Is one suspended note.
Then two girls:
They walk this way, up the hill,
And they laugh—one long Chord is made.
The High Plains Creoles are on their way:
Barbed twang Dobro, Spruce topped guitar,
Twinkling bells in the mandolin,
The big bass holding the bottom of the lines.
Do you ever find yourself
Alone in a room

In the middle of the night
And talk to yourself about the past
Until you hear so many voices
You have to tell
Yourself to shut it down?
Well, here I am, and
Shut it down,
But the voices come on
Until all the stories
In the graveyard are told
In the bright lights
Beyond the shadows
Of the grain elevator walls:
Right in full view of
The tall blue water tower
Under the rock and
Clay of this prairie valley
Flows a chain of lighted
Caverns and cathedrals,
And every memory
And moment is
Laid out in its own sacred room

Only an ancient
Soul can hear and understand:
Red, deep blue, black, green,
Yellow, and most esteemed white:
The color of snow, holiness, death,
The 24 note thick wind of the
High Plains Creole blues,
Or plain chant notes and
Slip-slid sting
And a slip slap beat
Of a single voice
In the wilderness guitar song

Summations are for courtrooms.
Here we need arguments
In the form of benedictions

The scorners say,
"The love in this town
Has only survived
For these barely 100 years"
But we say, "Look!
We have seen the WWI
Veteran limp across the
Waxed gold floor of the
High School Gym
On many Memorial Days"

See the pictures of drought?
Dust drifted on Main Street,
The fence lines buried
And the mythical blizzard
That entombed the County
In the blinding frozen white
Polar bear cold, WWII,
Low cattle prices;
The oil boom passed us by
Even the Holiday House
Finally burned down-
Bobby's brick bank
Is a museum these days,
But the clock on its corner
Above the street still
Keeps time with now-
The new bank is
A proud city fleshy dream.
We live 1000 years in 100-

We are a spot that
Lives slowly at the speed of light-
We move in love, slowly
At the speed of grass grown passion

***

(For Ron Vossler and the Vossler lady
Buried in Wishek ND last week)

At the grave by the grain elevators,
"Towers of the eye of god," Ron says, north of town
In the howling late March Jack rabbit wind,
Or on a cracked, perfectly Sharp-edged October day (sky
    edge to earth—
A straight seamless line of horizon in three directions)
I will make my argument:
I just make this town
Of eternal love out of holy mercy,
The real meaning of pathos, pity,
Ejaculations of wishful intents,
Words, to air, to silence-

Point out the dates on the stones,
Babies, crib deaths,
Mothers in childbirth,
Displaced veterans of
Washington's imagined, self-full-filling wars,
Power take offs, cars smashed on
Short curved gravel roads;
Drunkards, sinners, worm-eaten saints-

I will tell you: the chord holds strong
In the mad March Wind; this love,
The war cry of wisdom,

Wind from the wings of angels:
One word—love.

There we were that August:
Peggy and John Fielder,
My father, my wife, and friends
In a circle around Margie Gordon's
Grave—right next to Mrs. Vossler,
9 months early, 200 miles away,
Still the same day in the
Grasshopper's tall grass prairie eye
I know—I gently brushed him off my sleeve

This is a town of prodigal sons and daughters
We come and go and never really leave
Fatted calves are few and far between

There is so much of this prairie breeze,
This forgiveness that blows;
The ghosts of loving mothers and fathers
Are so subtle

And when a prodigal prods himself to leave,
One more is sure to return on the wings of
Some Alberta Clipper, a full snowed sail-

We take them in to the hot stove,
Meet the midnight freight from Nashville
Or Southern California
With our warm breathe smoking,
Wrap them in our arms,
Poach a wild turkey and pheasants too,
And call it New Years all over again-

***

In this town, when men and women
Fall far short of love,
They go to the Wolf Den
And howl out on vodka
Or to the Turkey Track to tout tequila,
Or old Rixen's Bar with the
Polka infected beer
(you drink fast, in polka time),
Or to the real Pheasant Lounge,
Where at the end of the longer day
The Windsor Watson's rest-

They drink the sorrow, an angry love,
Their self-damnations too,
Then go back home to each other's arms,
And ancient marriage bed of
Sagging springs and rising oak:
Confession at St. Vincent,
Where Mary, ever blue,
Even in the red state town,
Always understands,
Or the rock walled Lutheran,
The other judge on the hill,
Where Martin tends bar
At the 'Means of grace',
And when all else fails,
You try the Assembly of God
Where the collected congregations
Hear with joy the collected sins: AMEN,
And Jesus washes the failed heart away-

All too early, a year rolled around,
The retired farmers,
The sidewalk farmers—

8

("Retired means tired again,"
Says one feed capped wag)
Park their trucks in front
Of the Pheasant Café-
Sunlight rolls cross the
Plateaus to the east,
Rolls waves of light
On the dead in the grave yard,
Water tower, grain elevators,
The cold brick walls of the public school,
The early mass bricks of St. Vincent,
And daddy long legs water tower—
They all cast a long green Martian shadow
Out west like a pointed secret signal,
Across the valley and west again, again-

Light beats on the west side of Main Street
Where Bob Carvell sweeps his sidewalk
In front of the Rexall Drug,
And the smell of pistachios floats
On the speckled light
Out of the open doors, again, again
And mixes itself with the
Unearthly smell of
Jon Jones' bakery smells: all light, again-

That one morning,
I am there on my red bike,
Watching it all,
A summer Saturday-
God knows why-
I should have been home
In my mourning dove haunted bed-

But that day the dust from

Bob's waving broom is holy,
And the old German Russians
Process like monks
Through the doors of the
Pheasant Lounge
For the Eucharistic fire
Of sweet wine in old bellies-

Years later, Dick Halvorson,
Punster and jazzman poet,
Over a cool tomato beer,
Shows me where all the
Old men sat on the that day-

We lower bodies of dead loved ones
Into the ground as southern
Light is at its gauziest; it attacks our human graves-
It floats in blinding layers
Over the temple towers,
The wish for higher prices and surplus set against
7 years bad luck, low yields and income tax on air,
The Wheat King's cathedral coffers,
But we all get our own shares-

We lower the loved ones down,
But they only leave old skin
And bones in the satin-bedded space-
They have already taken leave
Of our weak and shortened eye-

All of our lives, the dead live with us,
Follow us as we live in that town,
Home with us at the whistle: curfew and noon,
Out on the swing sets with us at recess,
Home for roast beef suppers-

If we leave town,
Our dead come along,
All one with the air in a suitcase-
They whisper the joys, some admonitions,
Instructions, advice,
Until we come back home-

Then they ride on the hoods of brand new cars
As we drive into town on Highway 8,
Past the Pheasants and deer-
We look out through the eyes of our dead,
And we know where we are-
We can smell the Cannonball River from here-
We remember the Great Depression with fondness-

In those times of drought and religious doubt
We have been known to live on lard bread
And kill and eat any beast that moves,
Any critter that doesn't give milk or lay eggs-
In Hettinger County, small birds,
Jack Rabbits, snakes and wandering
Federales from Washington end up in stew,
Steamed with stray roots and many dry weed seeds-

We keep our primitive peasant pheasant loving vows
(Finally got the three p's to roll),
Give thanks for the meat we eat,
And when the rain comes,
And we're back to white bread, steak and eggs,
Green beans, tomatoes, the fruits of the gumbo gardens,
We remember the dry time with the minds and
Eyes of hungry, blues singing beggars-

***

When all things fail,
Our loved ones crawl
In to the whiskey council
Of the dark Wolf Den-
There is room there to snarl-

The veterans gather around,
Pinion him down
And then take a fast car
Across the border,
Past the Slim Buttes-
Antelope bound in tan, empty pastures,
Among the slow grazing herds of cattle and sheep,
And drop him off at old Fort Meade-

He takes his own cure there,
South of holy Bear Butte,
And when it works
The wounded soldier comes
Home from his latest war,
Skinny and full of silence
He might not show up in church,
But you bet he'll be ready
To haul the next victim south-

We have been the same Spot
For just over 100 years-
A few of us almost remember it all;
Some of us passed it along,
And I came here to connect it,
Imagine and sing the rest-

Imagination—don't doubt it;

It brought us across the water
And over here from the first—
And I don't mean sad sack
Divine right of Ferdinand Colombo and crew

There will be more than one History class
At the final "All Class Reunion",
Like summer itself is memory fried
In the fire of July and August days-

It is as if every soul in this town,
Including the souls of the sparrows,
All lived the same remembered ages,
And in the mote of God's eye, we do-

There are the maroon curtains in the
Mott Lincoln High School gym,
The veterans, cheerleaders,
Class B champion basketball teams,
The carnivals of the winter night,
Right before the snow blew in
In drifts as tall as Atlantic waves-

In fact, we remember every living thing
That any one in this small place has ever done,
And wish they'd done or wish to undo,
And we are smiling, too
In some small eternal way-

***

There is a little room
For every love and hate that made us
Thrive or fail-
It is not that we were real-

In fact we know we still are;
We are still here-
Sometime in some June we get together,
All those days when the prodigals return-
We blow our horns on Main Street,
Have a mass barbeque on the pavement,
And then even the one legged farmer will dance
Until the drumming of our feet will make some rain-

The High Plains Creoles will stomp out the Cannonball
    Blues,
And I will bellow them vocals out,
Like a northern-nasal-Elvis Zimmerman
Like a high on Water, Bread and Wine,
The words and notes will all be true-

I am trying to remember
What the playground is like
At the public school-

We needed no fences
Only the greasers and
Smokers strayed across the street,
And of course in those days
The playground was so huge:
A row of cottonwoods (Chinese elms?)
Along the eastern rim,
The soft powder diamond
With a wire mesh backstop that all the bad boys climbed,
Two sets of metal swings,
A little gravel and no concrete,
Yellow grass when the rain gave up,
And plenty of bare dirt for marbles, sticks,
Red Rover and tag-
Drifts were as hard as the principal's hand,

Or else as soft as a grandma's bosom
When the snow was too deep to drift—
A white field of fortresses, caves, secret alliance.
Times of clear brittle silent prayers-

At the top of a tall slide that silent
Janus faced Roman witched winter day,
My mittens stuck on the rail,
And I stood up and balanced,
High above the noise of noon in the town,
Blessed the four directions,
Breathed in white terror, joy—
I could see the curve of earth;
Love and the bell made me come back down-

We plated the town just north
Of Sitting Bull's summer camp,
A few miles east of deep black butte
Where his father died in battle
Against the longhaired swooping Crow

On the bones of the buffalo,
The treasures of the Hunk Papa people,
Buffalo bones inside teepee rings
(We seem to be blessed with their fate),
And the pastoral care of blue stem grass,
The rocks we harvest like fresh glacial eggs every spring,
Lignite coal veins,
The clans of birds that return
With the rocks every spring,
Meadowlarks melodrama in opera arias
On all of the fence posts again,
With operatic scales,
Robin's eggshell blues,
Red wing black birds do one-liner chuckles

And ride on thin, wind-bent reeds,
Holy hermits roosting over the slough-

The crows have learned English, too,
And on winter nights they
Meet to feast in the empty barns-

The county coyote named himself Jack,
In memory of the dead game and fish man
The deer are domestic,
The antelope read books of Russian origin,
Warm in the German Russian snow,
And the cougars are back,
Just to give a nice chill
To the long cold Indian nights-
The female dogs once more wear
Bonnets on Easter Sunday

Newly brown rabbits make
Deep designs in fresh grave yard grass,
Nuzzle the happy ghosts that come
To play with the rabbits around the stones,
And the puppies help the children sniff
Out the deep stained, dye kit Easter eggs-

The dead are peaceful, pleased, excited,
Primed with annual hope
And ready for resurrection-

The oil boom can't end all this,
Not even the soon to come drop in price
Of the sacred bushel of wheat-
The grass grew back, sweet on the
Packed down gumbo of great depressions-

They say we are shrinking,
But so is the Milky Way.
When we live small
We will stay small, only then,
But we are ready for the final great return-

We suck in our bellies right here on the Spot
We know more than ever, whatever we thought,
God forgot nothing; that was Washington boys,
And they rode awry on the long freight train rails
After they bought off the NPL-
We rise from the shroud that we thought was
Just sorrow, dirt, depression, war, brutal snow

***

The farther we grow away from youth in this place,
The more we see the passion left for old age and death-
We would have worried the sweaty small stuff less,
And known more worship in secret childish rest,

But we made ourselves busy with clothing, faces and hair,
And each other's bodies, blessings, and cars,
Called ourselves all grown up-
Now in our age we can feel the passion that lets
Us forgive our tear stained backward glance-

Let's move—Go in peace and serve the Lord, they say-
May we move through these days in one long benediction
In which we reach the space of God between our eyes,
Our lips, to see that we make one common, holy point-

The one armed drunkard
From south of town,
The stillborn child,

(you know what that means?)
In the empty house,
The wedding dress and
Soldier's mufti
Will/can dance back to life
Along with the still-borns'
Parents-

In the shelter belt
Of Russian olives
The pheasants all crow
Like the great cock of the sunrise
The old stone Lutheran Church
Across from the county courthouse
Counting house on the western hill-

We will rock with music
The marching band, Ernie and the Polka Kings,
The Remains, The Road Runners,
The Mavericks and Country Cousins,
Naomi with her foot on the metal of the
Pipe Organ pedals,
And the High Plains Creole's lead
The Musical musketry, the sprightly jig and reel—
Let the reel run backwards in ancient melody-

Runes and rolls that rock the main street, wide
As old brick St Vincent's new addition
Burst forth as the Beatles meet the Bach
In busted boogied up Latin Chant,
And East and West Mott meet
On Main Street down in the Cannonball Valley rift-
Even the stray dogs and cats will be family then-

The buzzards, chickens, crows and road kill

"...will be transformed, all in the blinking of an eye",
A glimmer in the chocolate mirror of the slow
Old River-

See, time is a desecration then, a faker's fart
At the speed of sound, and we in this
Town knew before Einstein that we move in the Word
At the speed of Easter light-

Light makes the universe bend the high string
Of the dobro's ascending and descending
Choirs of angel joy,
Of the wooden guitars we call our souls-

Light builds up those resurrection blues,
The mandolin breeze, the bass line bounce,
But the surprising gospel of This Spot tells us
That anything that can, will happen,
And, past facts, that anything already has!

I write these things down in some other summer,
Ten summers, 50 years after the stuttering start,
For my sister Enid Bern, and (she, who I feared)
Her living brother (he gentled the fear—
Now he is dead, in full light too) and Larry, Blessed
By Wisdom and the wolf to be—
Still alive to tell the Little Bad Lands tunes
And my mother, (ice cream at night, the Gospel of John,
Southern Comfort sours, Brandy and soda)
The creak of the ironing board and bard—
By God She presses the wrinkles of time
And cotton as straight as the Road to Zion,
That Belle from Reinke Corners, north!

You should see the picture of she and her

19

State Teachers College friends dancing
Through the trees on the inside cover of
Her old cracked college annual: beautiful
Ladies, Andrews Sister knockout smiles,
On the edge or December 19—?
She sang to Jesus; that tall girl danced
My combat crazy father back from WWII,
And my own dear Nel, Brendon, Jesse,
And your Come Lord Jesus daily Dose-

Our incarnate medicine bundle and cross:
Water, Word, Bread, Wine, tomb and womb in one,
Growing larger that the Lion of Judah, The Lion of
Empire, this Prairie Cougar of a Final harvest joy—
So great, Son of Woman, that you dwarf the Milky Way
    herself-

We, in this Spot, the word that sounds like the Canaanite
God of fertility, "Maat", well loved by Phoenicians,
Philistines, Jews and the like,
Sounds like "Mawt" – spelled as "Maat",
The bawl of the lonely Herford calf—
Ain't that a mellow moo?

Will all rise from Robin's eggshell blue?
(You say you didn't coin that tinkling
Copper line, sweet Nel,
but to my ears you did),
Hatched that last Easter Sunday,
Before we got/get stuck in the cosmic egg-

Mott, you spawned a song in me,
Fingers for bronze strings,
This prized guitar, Martin,
As in Luther,

The Band, in Bethlehem, Penn,
Near Jerusalem
By way of a German hand,
Amazon, Wisdom, Wonder-Woman mahogany,
Spruce topped, Christmas satin blond,
(Nel again, my music made flesh in you)—
Girl, you peopled my living and dreams
(If that sounds country, it is, saith—the bard,
Kris Kristofferson: twice named Christos, you see?)-
I hang my blues on a Great Northern Railway Moan,
A whistle announcing the promise
Of words that grow from heart-head to tongue, lung,
Gut-throat to ears—
Maranatha! Revelation! Next year? Jerusalem, Slim!

…Meanwhile, somewhere in Southwestern North Dakota
Bless you, blessed Spot—
Diminish that your Lord might increase,
And you in your dying may take in the whole Milky Way-

I quote St Thomas McGrath and say:
"North Dakota is everywhere…"
"Now? Now!" (St. James, "When The Music's Over" M.)

"Yah! Well, we better get going,"—caught in the doorway,
The portal to the Kingdom of Heaven come, we shuffle
Our feet on the porch steps and say the blessing again-

&&&&&&&&&&&&&&&

Another ending, as if there would be
In a world where poems are abandoned,
WH, deep Auden said-

En mi interior de guitarra hay un aire viejo,

21

Seco y sonoro, permadecido, inmovil
(In the hole of my guitar there is an old tune,
Light and still rich, deserted, so still)—my English

—After Neruda's "Sabor"/ "Taste"

The song of Phineas' Wife: a widow and a ghost

The Bearded Lady

We sat around the burned-out fire pit,
Still warm from the night before;
The trees outlined a perfect avenue,
With the fire pit in the center of
The avenue, north to south-
Someone said it was going to rain-
Someone said it was too windy to fish-
Then someone said,
"If you stand and listen on the path
Beneath the caraganas,
You can hear the buzzing of the bees"

That night a moon hardly rose above our heads,
Above the lake named for the woman
That even her husband barely knew-
We still don't know how to spell her name-
The darkness lifted itself on
Huge, gentle paws and stretched across the trees-
One robin faced his breastplate west,

And the circle of the sun flattened itself
Into golden layers of light against
The trees in the shelterbelt
And bronzed the orange chest of the bird-

The pheasant cock in the shelterbelt
Crowed like a rusty sword
Scraping against rough stones,
Or the blades of an old windmill
Screeching in the wind in the red
Sunset on purple and blue snow
As the wind makes the struts of the tower
Shudder again and again-

Something heavy lifted itself
From the tall grass in the trees:
A "prairie cougar" (Brendon says),
Tall waving yellow-white grass
In the deep orange light,
Or a crouching woman
Made of leaves, grass, trees
And the dirt from beneath the trees-

Bonfires began to light the
Vault of the avenue under the branches
From the edge of the road on the north side
All the way out onto the shore
Where the water continued to work
And roll against itself in waves,
And then, with a woman's grace,
Flex, and dance, its deep wet muscles
Pressed against the sand, rocks and clay
Along the shore-

***

God is a verb,
Action and actress,
And we receive water unwanted,
In the lifting and drowning waves-

In what way is life a gift?
It is given before we know it,
Cling to it or let it go again-
Incomplete, it comes in waves,
And we receive and act
And receive the act again-
The action comes from a
Mystery far out on the water,
Beyond our eyes,
The eyes of worshipers,
Dogmatists, empirical
Watchers and
Figures revealed on
Canvas, lighted screens and
The walls of ancient caves...
There is a beginning-
We see the middle-
There is no end
In "... ...World without end, Amen"

And then, the mystery seems
To take us, unwilling, willing, away:
The book of Genesis,
Stories of lions near the fire,
Words lost in the space
Between the electrons of
The atomic curve,
The bush that burns in Moses' brain
But never consumes itself: "I AM";

The Word of words in act and shape—
Beyond the words of Plato or John;
The ending Act of a new Beginning
In Revelation's end: "…Alpha, Omega…"

And what we might fear as judgment,
Fate, some destiny's endgame journey,
Is, in fact, Wisdom received for freedom…
She acts upon us, "…for freedom's sake",
Until even our acts are the expression
Of a majestic leap inside the lap of another womb-

The heresy, the witch-crafted dark thought,
Is to think that we are the primary
Actor and the source of the act-

The hope, the Kingdom's blessed female
Hand—Wisdom—comes when
We are brought to life, called in an act
That begins with Her first chanted
Aleph, and ends in the operatic shout
Of her final, new, "Ooh", omega-

***

The Blame of the Apple, Again

Miranda, what kind of freedom is it for you
To have a cancer tearing at you
When your twin, Sophia, is pronounced clean?
And who acts or acted; what choice
Was freely or not so freely made?

If you forget that you were once wretched and sick
Or merely a slave,

26

You become sick with slavery again
And ignore someone who is still a slave-

Where is the Wisdom that stops the knife?
The hunger, the sickness, the wound?
This would be freedom, we think…

—Or you, Jon Benet, again and again,
New DNA, the drama of false confessions
The needy world of the empty, violent men,
Photos on the world's web sites…

The pageant turns from beauty
To ropes, bruises, terror and death—

Or Dru, dead
for months on the banks of
The frozen and thawing Red River,
As dead as Ophelia,
Drowned in the pounding blood,
Crazy Alfonso and his knife?
What kind of stage for a god to work?
The cameras of a shopping mall parking lot,
The cell phone dead in Hamlet's hopeless hand,
DNA, fibers, dried brown blood…

The little girl gone with the momma's boy friend,
His suicidal stretch in the tomb of his own van,
The false death-walk of a wild life refuge,
The frustrated bloodhounds,
The angry, circling hunters,
And odd look in the mother's eyes
As she smiles and says,
"I am comforted," live, on the local news.
We know by then that she

Didn't go look for the girl for
Three days-
Even God only took that long to
Unwrap Jesus in the tomb-

Who rolls these lives
As if they were multiple dice?
What are the roles of the rolls, Sister Wisdom?
We have named them—
Chaos, nature, nurture, natural selection,
Sin, law, salvation, choice and grace-
Who measures the distance between these things?
Collections of desperate words are
Formed by word-wracked brains-
Use a yardstick, a scope or a scalpel-

When will the hands of the dead mothers
And daughters in this horrible mystery
Wipe the smart look off the Sanctified, or baptized
One time too many and/or the Academic
Statistical sophistical philosopher's
Satisfied, placid unfazed man-face faces?

Miranda, a twin to Sophia,
And the little girl gone—
Packed in her mommy's cheap suit case
In the ditch at the side of the road—
Beauty queen, lost girls,
Dru in the hands of the dead-eyed
Fifty two year old rot meat driven
"Sex offender"—what words!—
Who used the afternoon matinee
As an alibi?

Girls, is it time

To pitch your voices lower,
The grunt of the charging
Female Grizzly,
Or higher— a female cougar's scream;
Should you carry arms?
Learn to kick, gouge and bite
With the ancient power
Of birth against death?
Should you shoot first?

Why is the flag at half-mast?
The DNA didn't match-
The bear cages have all been filled-
Hollywood Moses waves his M16-
White House Idiots cheer-
And gun show talk show hosts,
Over-dosed on diet pills,
Stare the eye AM of the Universe down:
"...from my stiff, dead, cold fingers!"
Ah, come on boys,
Hold something else in your hands!
More than that flag is lowered half-mast-

We sit in our prime rate homes
Absorbing necrophiliac phantasies
Of G rated Nielson news
(I had a Saul Bellow quote here,
But out of respect for my decent dead,
I let him rest—read the book—)

"Jerusalem; Jerusalem; how many times?"
Those are the words of Nazareth Slim-
Miranda is welcomed back home-
The genetic tick in her adrenal gland
Is clear for now, for sure, for now;

So close this clean bill of health-
The little girls are still gone missing-
The mother's TV smile is on my mind:
(The "Dead Man" in the van will know),
The bloodhounds at the wildlife refuge,
And I still sniff and howl for clues-

Say, there's Dru's murderer on local TV:
If, then death;
If not then life without parole: this time-
The bear cages are all full-
There on the screen:
A pretty picture of a pretty Dru
Super-imposed above his shoulder.
The 52 year old convicted felon
With the empty face I hope no one
I love will ever have to face alone
See the look on the faces in the room
When I say, out loud,
I am sinful enough
To pull
The switch,
The trigger,
Release trap doors,
Or do the injection right now
Call it an act of charity-

Act, respond; how do we respond?
Life in death hands out a death or life-
What makes murder the act of
A slave,
When the slave thinks the act will
Set him free,
And the victim,
Is at his feet again,

As innocent as a deer?

Big old bearded GOD and DARWIN,
You both look like stinkers to me!
Or do we claim the moves for you
That we won't claim for brute
Accident and our own dark
Choices blamed on chance-
Our pride in our fall made
Those choices for us long ago?

Too much of a theme here,
It makes for a story,
And this is not, at all;
Do we think that I might? Know
Where—action, response,
Life and death slave or free—

Where is this headed?
These words add up to what
I do when I am lost
On the ragged edge
Of hopelessness and grief-

Why a poem?
Words don't make poems
Of sorrow, insomnia,
The grey gauze sky,
And the same taste on the
Teeth and tongue
At 5 am, after the
Car tires squeal in the street
In front of the house,
After the sounds of
Breaking glass and

The crazy drunk tank
Laughter
From the darker shadows
Inside the
Bass booming shadow
Car-
Language pushed to
Painted metaphor
Makes it somehow human-
Neruda, McGrath,
How do we chart the
Catastrophes of human
Fury that carry
No political name?

***

I seek the other side,
Where what I cannot fathom,
The horrific soul sucking
Terror of the victim,
Or the dead-handed
Inability to feel pity
As the hand grasps
The hair,
The right hand that
Holds the penis, pistol,
Razor, knife…

How can even six senses
Push behind to the other side…
Other side of what?

The other side of horror—
Where is the great "I AM",

The burning bush that
Is never consumed,
That movement, motion,
The theophany that takes
The hands
Of ten million mutilated
Women,
Body, cunt and soul,
And heals, honors, holds
In glory?
These things are beyond the
Speed of the human
Brain
The brain cannot
Comprehend
The horror or the holy-

In the rape, mutilation,
Torture, and murder trial courtrooms
Of this planet,
An old woman should stand,
Still as the hawk in the tallest
Branch of the oak,
And read Proverbs 8 aloud-

The burning bush that cannot be consumed
At the foot of the holy mountain
Opens into the womb of star light-
Fire, roaring cosmic juice and joy-
Take off your shoes, son of man;
You stand on your mother's womb-
We fear the thing between our thighs
When we should fear
The space between our ears,
The thundering dark

Encased in every human skull-

***

Late August (2007?),
Mindy Morgenstern,
The Valley City student,
Met the hands that
Broke the holy vessel
In the doorway
Of her living room-
How to handle our local news
When the horror comes home
From the alleys, wars,
And ugly dreams?

Small town strong, New Salem,
The home of dairy
Farms and prairies
And the sweet silly
Holstein of the sacred cow
On the hill on the shores of I-94...

Here's a PowerPoint stream of 10-second shots:
Little girl, horse back in a baseball cap,
Homecomings, proms, and parties,
The smallest events and the graduation—
Surrounded by a place, a space, the small town,
The long lines of friends, family, faces;

And always the striking dark girl in the
Picture, accidental, perfect, west river beauty;

Salem, in the Bible, a holy town,
Salem, the witch trials and Hawthorne;

New Salem, North Dakota,
A fertile place to redeem holy names
Where the grass is good for dairy cows,
And the local community boosters
Raised money for a giant fiberglass Holstein
To mark the town on I-94-
And, my friend, pull over and visit-
This thing ain't a golden calf-

The police ask for leads
To catch the man,
Who it turns out,
Passed the security check
That allowed him
To work in a county jail-

She was stabbed to death;
I will not picture the entrance points
(Was she raped?
How can we not remember,
Or why would we remember?
We are not producing 48 Hours here);
And then doused in cleaning fluid.
Moe, the jailer with the rap sheet for rape,
Left some prints and a good deal of DNA
Underneath the dead woman's nails-

{About this time, Jasmine, a folk singer friend of mine,
Tells about a veteran, Security Forces (retired)
He sat near her in sociology class-
He says, one day,
"There is no such thing as rape;
It's an excuse girls always use"

Dru, Ophelia of the Red River,

Mindy, merry maid,
Won't you make his excuses?}

Gibbs ends up getting to go to trial twice:
The second is held in Grand Forks.
The Herald says,

"In the first trial the jury was evenly split on whether Gibbs, 34, killed Morgenstern, 22, of New Salem. Authorities said Morgenstern was strangled with her own belt, stabbed with her kitchen knives and covered with cleaning fluid. Prosecutors said DNA evidence found under Morgenstern's fingernails and on her shirt proved that Gibbs killed her.

Gibbs attorneys argued that the DNA likely came from a doorknob in the apartment building where both Gibbs and Morgenstern both lived.

Gibbs is slated for trial Sept.17th for six felony charges he faces amid accusations that he sexually assaulted five female inmates while working as a jailer.

He also faces a trail for the 2004 rape of a Fargo woman, a date for which has not been set." (GFH Vol.91, no. 203)

Two pictures with the article, top center, show Gibbs, shaved head, frown, angry jutting jaw in profile, so he seems to be facing Morgenstern. She, from what might to be a school picture, faces you head on; dark hair pulled back, perfectly rounded face, half smile, dark eyed and lovely. How many versions of their story can those two photos create? It doesn't matter. She is dead. There is only evidence. Whatever a jury says, justice will not be done. Justice is not a possibility, and Moe has been wandering in and out of the system that is supposed to stop violence against women for a long time now. He already has that dead look in his eyes, yet:

The day I see the picture
Of the Black man accused of murder
As he frowns across the white
Newsprint space between his picture
And the picture of the dead woman,
Still fully alive, of course, in print,
I find this colored frame from a
1943 Classics Illustrated Classic Comic:

Against a tropical background,
Next to what appears to be white pillars,
We see two figures; Uncle Tom
In a blue suit and white shirt,
And Eva in purple,
Wrapped in a green blanket,
Her blond head on
A big white pillow-
She is cradled in Tom's arms-

She says, "Uncle Tom,
Would you like to be
Back in Kentucky
With your family?"
Tom says, "I would,
little Eva, but I can't"
When irony is too much for politics
I put on Hendrix and cry

***

About this time a year ago, when summer was too dry
for decent wheat, too hot and muggy to be enjoyed, a woman
named Emily was walking home in the residential area in the

northwest part of town where many college students rent apartments. She turned and saw a man in a dark, hooded sweatshirt, hood up, walking behind her. She grabbed her car keys from her jeans, and as he started to move up, move in even faster, she ran into and apartment building and rang a doorbell. Someone answered the door, stepped outside with her, and they saw the man in the sweatshirt run across the street.

A few days later a father looking for the daughter he hadn't heard from for too long drove in from a small town nearby, unlocked her apartment and found her dead. She had been raped and murdered. A man in a black hooded sweatshirt had been seen in the vicinity around that time.

One early morning that week, after I had left the windows locked and the air conditioner on, I was sitting on the couch by an open balcony door drinking coffee—for some reason I notice my two grandmother's Bibles on the loveseat next to a Rolling Stone magazine with a sexed-up, sloppy, lurid picture of a faded, jaded, former teen, now rated a female pop star. What was I reading last night?

That same day a friend asked me why I agreed to write songs for a musical extension of 'The Vagina Monologues' the previous winter. I pointed to the Bibles, the Rolling Stone, and said, "Can you make a connection between my songs, these Bibles, and this Rolling Stone cover?" He smiled. Now, in the summer of 2008, I write one sentence as simply as I can. I do not wish to appear ironic. I am angry and horrified. No one has been arrested for the murder. Her funeral was one year ago.

Where do these horrors come from? Alien intrusion? A few years back a man suffering from Alzheimer's, early stages, took his wife out to an abandoned farm a few miles southwest of the town where I grew up, killed her, stuffed her in a barrel and then went upstairs in an abandoned building and killed himself.

I overheard this story at a table in the "Café Court" of the local mall: "His best friend was the sheriff, had to go and get him, driving around town in a pick up, 20 degrees outside, him in his underwear. They found his wife dead in the kitchen, one bullet hole in her head, but he had beaten her up first. He was the best shot I ever met."

Here is one from two years ago, and I can't tell you who told me. The children don't know what happened. "She was his golden girl, almost too close to perfect, so bright, so sunny, a joker, beautiful—then she got MS and she shriveled and shrunk for 20 years; crutches, wheel chairs; he had to bath her and feed her. Then he smothered her. When the town cop wouldn't arrest him, he got in the car and drove off an embankment. His kids thought he killed himself when he found her dead.

Spring, 2007: she was running with her back to me, down University Avenue, headed east, caught in the head lights of several cars, including mine. I thought, well she feels safe and free, running at this time of night. Her long thick ponytail bounced left to right on her shoulders. Then as I pulled even, she staggered, ran out in front of me as I hit the brakes, then turned, looked into my headlights and yelled. My window was down. She said, "Get him! Bobby!" and stumbled to the other side of University. A cop was coming from the other direction. He pulled over, got out of his car and ran after her as she ran up the steps and through the door of a little white house. I have no idea how it ended. After two more patrol cars pulled up, I drove away.

I don't know what I had expected, maybe an apologetic smile as I slowed down for her to cross the street. She was bleeding from a cut on her forehead, she was weeping, and instead of a smile, I got the half-peeled grimace of agony.

***

Between Finite and Infinite, part II

Come as a Child (a children's song)

Come down the street in a lop-sided grin
Like he invented a cure for some original sin-
Come as a child, or don't come at all-

They out to get you, non? Oh, Paranoid?
These are the people you need to avoid-
Come as a child, or don't come as all-

Walk in the room, wrapped in a sheet,
Black combat boots, stuck on his feet-
Come as a child, or don't come at all-

Now when he stands at the pearly white gates
He knows all of the sinners, glad-hands the saints-
He will not have too long to stand there and wait-

Like some young fool, he stands out in the rain-
If he were here, he'd do it again-
Come as child, or don't come at all-

***

A Metaphor Some Women Know: Legend of the Deer

On highway 22, near New England, North Dakota, at let's say, late autumn dusk, although it could have been spring or summer. Think Hawthorne, not for the landscape, which is nothing like where we are—think Salem/New England gothic without the trees—gothic in the spookish way the light rolls west to east across the yellow grass for the shape of this true story. The car rolls down the road, the road rolls over the hills, and the hills roll on, with the long blue shadows, incredibly long and elegant shadows, considering that this is supposed to be flat land, so you have to wonder how shadows could grow so long.

Two cars, one headed north, one headed south, draw parallel to each other on that highway. There are a total of three women in the two cars. As the cars pass, two of the women in one car might glance out at the lone woman in the other car, or not. Maybe they are talking. Then, out of those shadowed, rolling wide-open spaces, a deer appears. The deer leaps and flies out of the darkened, scoria-streaked sky. The deer bounces off one car, flies through the driver's side windshield of the other car, straight through, out the back window. Of course the cars careen around. One of them hits the ditch. One deer and one woman are dead. The other two women are left alive.

I will come right out and tell you. This is the way I experience the violence of this world against woman. This is the pain, grief, love, fear I feel for every female in the world, with the knowledge that the face beneath the black hood could have been mine, or the face of any man I have ever known. This is what I know about the logic of sexual violence against women. I cannot make it into a poem.

***

    I have been sitting in the motel room in Fargo, North Dakota, and in a motel room in Moose Jaw, Saskatchewan, thinking about space, wide open out here, violence, women, focused and unfocused hatred, projectiles (one deer, bullets, knives, fists, fingers, and of course the penis). For centuries the projectiles have remained remarkably constant. So has the behavior of men towards women. What about motivation?

    In two motel rooms, the hours passed as I considered these things. Outside, years will pass, and the acts of violence will pass too, come and go, while the women and the men all come and go, caught in all the acts. I looked at prints made of landscapes of abandoned farms on the walls of two motel rooms several hundred miles apart. Sin is omnivorous, banal, lusty, controlling, dominant, and as focused as a deer through a windshield or the desperate, furious thrust of a raging man's penis. There is so much space in this world, for beauty and for violence.

***

    This night, the wind rips clouds into shreds and sends them like shafts of translucent glass between the full moon and my eyes. The white ball of the moon pulses as I stare at it: This caused by my eyes, not by the moon itself. The street below the balcony is brightly lit, so any shadow is equally dark. The body of the little girl has not been found. The rapist/ murderer, maybe a man in a black sweat shirt with the hood pulled up, is still free, maybe out walking tonight: his mouth is open slightly as he walks, and with some part of his brain cells totally aware of what he wants, the other part of his being spouts words, whispered or silently, but fully

42

formed into thoughts, from some bank of sick cells saved and nurtured from the horror of some sublimated act of violence, some terrible pain, and in the thoughts, formed into images, there is fury, and the fury will be directed in a sudden, complete act of destruction against some woman, a woman with no idea that the violence is on the way.

***

Students and Trees: Statements for Further Investigation

-The black hooded sweatshirt disappears in the empty spaces of night between the street lamps.
-The student is found dead in her apartment in the NW part of town.
In the middle of an attack, bright headlights in his chosen parking lot interrupt the perpetrator. The young woman, another student, escapes. The driver and she say the attacker was wearing a hooded sweatshirt.
-On his birthday, a former university student is murdered at his party by another former student. This summer, I watched his mother as she watched the trial of the two accused murderers. I sat on the couch, watched her on the news and looked out the balcony windows, over the trees of the valley towards where the murder happened last summer—about two miles away.
-In the biting, skull pressing muggy heat of one unbearably hot august afternoon, all the fine old trees along the University Avenue, next to the university of course, where students walk at night, come down to beaver buzzing chain saw.

How in this world can our bones ever feel any safety, in the in the holy armor of the sacred groves or in the wide-open space of prairie? Earth, woman, tree, man—where is the mercy?

***

There is a Deadly Danger in Pity and Speed

I saw a female coyote loping along in a ditch on Highway 83, just a few miles south of the small city where we live. This is unusual, although last week two female moose broke up the pee wee games at the local diamonds for over an hour, and two nights ago, two young does and a white tail buck larked and grazed 100 feet from our house in our neighbor's front yard. We don't see coyotes or cougars right along the road. For some reason I thought this lone traveler was a she.

When I pulled into a small town south of there, a quick, hard summer storm blew up from the west and sent tumbleweeds rolling along the empty railroad tracks. There was none of the rain that comes at that time of year, the end of May, just dirt, wind, weeds rolling along the rails running beside the road, and then a bit of hail.

Two days later on a Sunday morning as I drove back north, I slowed down for a large bit of road kill along the northbound lane. It was a coyote.

***

In the summer of 2008, Miss America fell on stage at the pageant when her "4 to 6 inch" high heels got caught in her evening gown. The Morning Show brought in a woman, an expert on how to buy and wear these shoes.

An old woman down the street from me was sweeping

glass off the sidewalk in front of her door, stooped, in an apron, broom in one hand, and pan in the other. She looked up at me, as if I had an appointment, nodded and said, "This damned dust pan is broken." She was wearing tennis shoes.

***

No, he needed to know her name. Unbelievable as she was, she didn't seem strange—no halos or organ music. He even wondered why he couldn't relax and let her just be here. If her name came to him, then good. –Reynolds Price

Now a woman is a fighter
Rather White or African
A woman is a woman, she
Has miracles for her man – Laura Nyro

Sometime after my mother died,
Suddenly
(We blessed and thanked her, but not enough),
I realized that I am a man with
An invisible body
It is located somewhere in
The muscles of my heart-
It began to grow the night
After the afternoon she died
In a great wind that blew
Me all the way back home-
There are senses, I swear,
Inside my ear drums,
And so they hear the sound of
Every baby ever born
From every womb that
Ever birthed and

Every gate that ever
Split and bled for life-

Sisters, how do we learn
The mercy and violence of
The birthing womb?

Forgive us, mothers,
As we remember the
Girl caught and raped
At 8 am on a winter day
When the she thought
She was on her way to work-

Forgive us, mothers of grief
And teach women and men-
Show mercy, sisters of pain
And teach women and men-
We are made from each
Other's tears-
We are strong in each other's trust-
A man is a man in a woman's hand-
A man is beast when he makes a fist-

Bless us, mothers and fathers of grief
And teach us to treasure the light
Behind the eyes of every creature we know-

&&&&&&&&&&&&&&&&

Never enough—it will go on, and we will
Despair or pray—even the earth can weep
I have seen grasslands weep after the rain-
It will go, and we will still learn to laugh,
Like the Pheasant Hens and their Cock

In the trees an hour before the sun sets-

I use metaphors, and I thank Marian Moore-
Metaphors are real things
That imagine redemption in songs
About a real garden
Where even toads are beauty,
Snakes speak but never bite,
And Eve walks out in the cool night
While Adam walks along, or sleeps-

***

The Bearded Lady: a vision
(For Larry Woiwode)

He said, "My name is Homer"
As he slid up to the bar
He said, "I play the harp"
I said, "I know what you are"
"I wrote the Iliad and Odyssey"
I said, "Helen and Penelope?"

Pay your ticket, Homer, see?
You must kiss the Bearded Lady

He said, "My name is David
I made blessings on the harp
I put mad king Saul to sleep
When his fury went too far"
I said, "You killed Uriah
And stole Bathsheba's heart,

And now you face it David: see?
You must kiss the Bearded Lady"

Wisdom waits at the city gates
She says, "Come learn you fools
Come and eat my bread and
Drink my wine for free"

When I was a newborn
The angels came to me
They sang, "Boy now you will
Play the harp,"
But I heard the word "guitar",
So all these years I
Sing the blues
My inner eye can see,

Soon I kiss the Bearded Lady

Wisdom waits at the sheepfold gates
She says, "My lambs know me
No wolf or thief can steal them away

Kneel and kiss the Bearded Lady"

Ichabod, kid brother, accidental committer of matricide, remembered in name only.

Prelude:

You Gotta Be Hard-Forged To Live Up Here

Get this dude! For no where to go,
In summer-wear in the metal
Of Janus's werewolf two headed howl—
When The Music's Over
Blasts out his iPod
And he's only 16 years old
Thinks Jimmy M is Val Kilmer,
Who ever he was—
Many ain't got no culture,
But it's all right, phat,
Every body must get cloned—

January 6, 2011, I said to my self,
"Remember! Then you revolt against all death!"

If my life is one long battle
In a variety of keys and counter–lines,
(Remember to revolt against all death)
I am the loyal opposition
Until balloons, umbrellas, tea cups,
And all other magical implements dominate
The places darkness has always ruled

Remember, and even if I forget,
You might remember yourself

      ***

Part I:

———————————————

This is a collection of voices, from St Albans, UK, New York City, to Minot. Phone calls, interviews, news broadcasts, and E mails were all used for this piece. A small amount of organization went into it. If I were a real editor, I would call it a dated journal from a select group of people on the subject of the flood. But the point of it, for me, is that it makes one voice in telling itself. It is roughly chronological. Any of my particular comments will be prefaced with the word "Editor". About 100 people contributed to this piece. Most of them know about it.

—Rick Watson, July, 2011 (August 2012), Springfield Avenue, Minot North Dakota

***

I think there's a found poem in that... I have similar thoughts. I'm reminded of James Michener's interest in offering a brief but profound glimpse into the geologic immensity of our place and context, as a reminder that the little story he is about to unfold is, as Annie Dillard would depict, like grains of sand, small pieces of our earth that have undergone incomprehensible changes. That puts our little situation in a clear and modest perspective, one that I doubt many people contemplate seriously. There was a woman who wrote an editorial criticizing our Earth Day event and the campus clean up. She implied naively that taking care of the earth really doesn't matter: that what matters is our (hers in particular, I suppose) everlasting life and the meaning of Easter (a sacred day heralding Christian salvation), not the meaning of our the Earth or any need to protect it, assuming we have the conceit that we have an ability to do that. I guess one could say that it does move beyond hydrology to theology. Whatever it does, though, it's pretty darn interesting and curious that any of us can think or imagine that we can understand much of it, no less create some kind of concept of a grand caregiver. Water has a grand power.
    –received E Mail

Water runs down hill, finds a way down hill—observe the water—the latest water levels out of Lake Darling—Darling?

...just re-read those last two lines of yours—Our original sin was to be arrogant enough to think we could see the creation as God sees it—God's original sin was, if the Genesis story were true, to tell us to take care of creation—"dominion" is a poor translation from the Hebrew. "Custodian/gardener" is closer to the original meaning—what a concept! Look what we have done: We are the grand care givers!!!!! I am watching images of the water even as we speak—is the whole valley in water?

Ten feet higher than the '69 flood: '69?
—How high's the water grandma?
—I hope it washes this house away this time—
—Don't forget that picture, and the woman who speaks
those words
            —KXMC News

It really breaks my heart to think of all the fine people who
have lost their homes and have to be displaced. I saw two
beautiful little girls—maybe ten years old or so—twisting in
their hula hoops in the darkness of The Dome floor last
night, trying to smile. The father, whose face expressed sheer
defeat and numbness, was standing nearby sipping coffee.

I used to be heartened by the Christian notion of Dominion
and its various interpretations of the sincere care accorded to
our earth and to animals. I'm less so now.
            –E Mail

—look at that marker on the light pole!
This time the water will be ten feet higher, ten feet higher!
            —KXMC News

Editor:

Iris the Humane librarian
was in the flood and her
house is an island on the TV
news in the middle of the river
the library books are safe in small
towns all around the state,
towns with names like Anamoose—
She says, "tell you hi!" and
mentions that some students

52

helping evacuate the books
found an old pair her red shoes
she hadn't seen in awhile

These are things we remember
when our homes are gone

—Didn't lose the fight—the fight's still going on—who or
whom are we fighting—(in the life we live with nature, it is a
great mistake to assume that nature acts in a manner that a
human being can comprehend nature—the same thing goes
for the great mysterious talk about the supra-being we name
God. Human sentimentality and pride insist that God is a
person, male or female—we talk about Mother Nature—
nature may have mothered the human race, or God may have
molded us from red clay (Genesis), but we do not, as a planet
or a race, have a mother or father that we can describe in
human terms. If "it" and "its" will and purpose can be
described in human terms, She/He/It is not a god. This river
is water, not a god, and this flood is NOT GOD'S WILL!

—So to fight nature, as in a river, or argue or define god, is all
sentiment and human self-interest—I do not know what we
will do—that home was paid for; it was my retirement; now
what?

—I felt like an idiot, so far away, unable to help, writing
checks to the Red Cross, and dripping tears on the Facebook
page
                    — E Mail

—Minot is open for business—the battle against the Mouse
—a slow motion disaster—a slow moving prairie tsunami—
how far is my tongue shoved into my cheek?
                    —KXMC News

— The Corps of Engineers and the rest of us, do not know as much as we need to know. After this flood, big decisions will be made about how we live in this valley—If we act the way we should, we could learn to live here with the water, in peace. If we don't make wise choices, we may continue to live here, but we will suffer again some day when nature chooses to let this amazing river loose. We study Hydrology and Geology, but this flood is also a matter of theology. A small town boy, familiar with the high plains and a prairie river called the Jordan said, "The wise man built his house on a rock."

—The fight is with our selves, battling with our ego. Only humans would be so stupid, and then so vain to cover their idiocy with ego and technology. I suppose we'll be fighting each other. They think they're fighting the Mouse, or the Missouri, but these aren't opponents. Try arguing with a stone. They're not interested in arguments. The Mouse and the Missouri will be here long after we're gone, and if it takes 1000 years, it'll weather away all our concrete, and it will be the most beautiful sight I could ever imagine. I have a really hard time not feeling nihilistic about all this. It's hard for me to feel sympathy for people as a whole.
      —E Mail

—Nature is for the time being, currently, winning out—this is a marathon, not a sprint in the battle against the river
      —KXMC News

—kid: Where's the bridge? Mom: Under water. Kid: Where's the grass? Mom: It's gone. Kid: Who took it?
—rivers bring people together—It was the rain that caused it.
      —KXMC News

—Did it rain all winter? We had to let the water go—Why didn't you let it go sooner? We are frantically fighting this flood—This is a fight to retain our dignity

—"Flood Fight 2011"—Mother Nature has reared up her head
        —KXMC News

—Water keeps going up and up and up. I hear it's flooding in Bismarck, too. I guess I am even more of a nihilist than Shawn Sipma (he really is), but I suppose no matter how much flooding we get in how many places, we'll still never learn. It's not as if they'll say, "Oh, oops, guess we won't build here." They'll just build and pave and dike and dam even more, and they'll talk about how it's so great for the economy and how there's no unemployment, never mind it's not locals doing the job, never mind the locals have to pay rent they can't afford due to huge influxes of people. "Shawn Sipma is such a downer," says Mary. "He even has to detail the lackluster qualities of the floodwater's coloration. Tom just sits and listens, grimacing. He seems grumpy and jumpy, like he's been told if his voice goes above a certain timber his chair will eject him."
        —E Mail forwarded (HAHAHA —She was watching the flood coverage on the Internet.)
        —(St. Albans, in the British Isles)

—Oaks grew in the coulees above the Sweet Briar Creek where I learned to swim at age six at the first crossing with Mom and the other kids. I always thought they were so exotic because the acorns wore these little caps that you could take off and put back on. That's a big deal for a little kid. I didn't have Barbie to dress, but I had a pocketful of acorns. Only their own hats would fit though. We're going to replace our green ash if (when) the borers come, with oak.

And C—— was showing me pix from the flood in the woods and he said do you know what this is? Is that cottonwood seeds? Yes he said. Floating on that stinky dirty water were fluffy white seeds for the next generation—now that's a nativity scene I can wrap my heart around. So if it means we don't graze or winter down there, if that's what it takes, that's what we won't do. And there were a few high places that actually stuck out of the water, so maybe some will make it. And of course I told him that the cottonwoods would die, C——, and he knew—it was in the paper.

—E Mail
—(South of Mandan North Dakota on the Heart and Missouri Rivers)

—big problem here is water, dirty, clean, pressure, lack of pressure—human pride hath writ disaster with its ass in the ink—

—the meeting last week, City Council, Corps, Guard, FEMA, Etc. — on Tuesday…wanted to run 'business as usual'— made me want to gag…they have no idea of the devastation to people's lives …we're doing nothing for DAYS, but just watching online, and they wouldn't let them go help! It was disgusting…we needed the help before the river rose. This takes years to recover from (I'm a survivor of the GF flood) …people's bank accounts will be drained along with the river. Yes, I hope the city does a huge buyout plan and makes parks and walking paths along the river…this won't be the only flood. They better prepare for more!

—"Maybe I am insanely dim and unconcerned, I don't know I'm sort of terrible and find the whole thing alien. Something happening somewhere else in the world... okay.... well you lost me at something. No one's died yet though? That's pretty impressive. We just have to have a minor heat rise and the

old people drop like flies. Like over these last two days probably 200 old people in St Albans got heat strokes, not even kidding, we're a susceptible bunch. Or a small gust of wind and some kid will be blown into a thorn bush and bleed to death— WHY AM I FINDING THIS FUNNY? I guess it's not exactly the death thing since they managed to evacuate the area, more the whole loads of buildings and stuff being destroyed, no water thing, hmm. If that happened to St Albans, man, we'd just be useless; I can't imagine us ever putting it back together again. We'd probably not have even got out of there and everyone would have become turgid from absorbing lots of water and preserved for hundred of years to come, like big bulbous water bombs with taut human skin instead of rubber, sort of like Pompeii but more peculiar. We could ship the bodies over to Minot for a supply of drinking water." (St. Albans is a small, ancient city in the British Isles)
     —E Mail

—the pictures of the flood, individual, personal water photos taken over a wide area of the valley, began to show up on "Flood Tracker" www. Something other, technology, as it has come to be called, in a "Social networking" way, made words, even E-mails, move over, and maybe even take a back seat. In a mess like this, almost as visual as it is emotional, metaphors, aphorisms, cries of pain, and slogans can be hammered by one photo after another on a computer monitor. One person said, "I want to see the pictures; I am tired of all the talking heads." Add 10,000 photos to the web, and you have a pictorial novel, a non-plotted narrative that can be constructed and de-constructed by anyone with a laptop. And the story can be told, re-told and intimately edited again and again. All these files and piles of digital images add a whole sensual dimension: simple narrative, dialogue, words of opinion and judgment, and human explanations might become a kind of meaningless thing, a second best way to face the fact of the matter of this sad, massive valley of water and wrecked human hopes, dreams and history. Imaginative and expository language may have met its match.

—Christianity, side by side with booster boy capitalism, has been an essential ingredient to the ups and downs of human culture on Mouse River since the 1890's: Protestant, Lutheran, Roman Catholic and now, Mormon—they all get into the act. The odd marriage of church and economic state in the form of boom and bust booster capitalism here in the Magic City is a book in itself. How will it play out in this chapter, and will anyone have the nerve to write about it?

—It's a kind of beast of a story—there are Hummers parked on my street—I have a door and a bed to sleep in—How do we find the stories? ...One TV reporter reports another as saying, "Go out and find people living in someone else's home." Where? , She says. The other reporter says, "They're all over!" She comes back with one piece introduced as "...a tale of two cities", north and south, divided by the huge river. It is about 3 and 1/2 minutes long—a kind of TV news novelette. "We have no home to go to," the woman in the story says. She is high and dry with "...no home to go home to"; her voice and facial expression are carefully controlled, her sorrow, subtle and huge. "—Our house will have to be demolished—I feel bad imposing—try and remember they (possessions) are just things—help somebody else and move on—remember he (God) gave you everything, and he can take it away."

—A man at a campground is glad to speak outside the bathhouse. He is haggard, worn by shock, and now grief: "...don't blame God because we can't build big enough dams or stay out of the river's way…there's only so much you can take before you hit the wall…what an amazing feat, in such a horrific way, what mother nature can do…I have no idea what to do next; I may not even have a job when I get back."

—Another guy tells a story I have heard 20 times or more: "I was wondering how I could ever get this stuff out, and I said a little prayer, and when I turned, 3 guys got out of a pickup with a big trailer hitched to it (Mennonites from Manitoba), and they emptied out my house in 45 minutes Wednesday before I had to be out."
—KXMC News

—a young national guardsman says, "Sure you need a life vest", and I (a truck driver) say, "What am I gonna do with that?"—Not many words you can say that can add to what you are seeing—

—Numbers that had no intrinsic meaning to any one but a hydrologist take on mystical significance: 1561.8-1559—one week of water makes numbers matter—like 1885's highest recorded crest was 1555, or two weeks at 1554 in 1969 —"How Long" and "How High" become sing-song mantras.

—FEMA has cleared Ward County for individual assistance —this is what we call and extended crest—"…help you in the process of getting back to your home…(not in rebuilding your home)"—Federal funds are limited too—well you don't see people marooned on roof tops like in New Orleans; we have the North Dakota spirit…
—KXMC News

"Boil the dam water!" becomes comic relief, flood relief and then a "T" shirt sold on the 4th of July in the only city park not under water; The Scandinavian Heritage Park; The name of the place and its shrines and buildings will tell ethnic mythology and give you some irony, if you still want some. —Bring it to a rolling boil for at least one minute—

Countless times, day and night, the video camera pans out, from east to west or west to east, from on top of one of several high buildings. We are shown the eerie beauty of the flood, north central North Dakota, and down town Minot before and with the coffee shop latte color of the flooded river.

—We have a flood warning for several counties east of Minot, from Harvey to Wilton—(the Mouse River turns and heads back north to Canada far north of the counties in the warning. The rain wants to play with the river.)—

—Someone reads in a late spring issue of the New York Times Book Review, a story about Einstein and Bohr as they sit around and snip at each other early in the 20th century, argue and "Ach" back and forth over which of them knows the meaning of what reality "is": quantify, objectify, typify it better than God could do it. Up here in the flood, a decade after some misguided followers of Mohamed remodeled Manhattan, in a time when all US Presidents are suddenly church-going born again god smackers, in the denial filled aftermath of New Orleans, the AIDS epidemic, victory in the Middle East, Reality TV, Super Bugs, and the de-constructed, re-constructed Mortgage, Stock Market madness, as we suck the last oil from the earth like a bunch of petroleum zombies, we better know that reality, as we humans describe it, isn't enough. We might wish that God weren't just a cute old word. By the way, the writer of the little bit you just read also heard that Einstein defined insanity as the same mistakes repeated over and over with the same negative results.

—"We had our own website for the flood"—sentiment doesn't make the river go down—we cannot have dominion over the works of creation—

—Religious literalism, Pop Social Darwinism, Multi-national corporate empiricism, consumer driven materialism all break down when a river floods—does the God, the dam builders, big business, the consumer cause the flood? Whose will is it? What religion in Minot ND teaches us to believe that God wills suffering, pain and loss?

—(two weeks ago at a press conference) "Two weeks and the water will be back in its banks. Then the real struggle begins." —New Orleans Red Cross worker: The mud and debris bake in the sun and heat and turn to concrete over every square inch the flood covers.
        —KXMC News?

—Press conference last week: We will get through this; the river has crested. But realize folks that we have gone from a crisis into a long haul, a long-term catastrophe.
        —KXMC News

—Father Time ran out of seconds and mother nature surged in—since we live on this street (points at sign) we call this "Nightmare on Elm Street"—graffiti on a concrete pillar (Broadway bridge? —the viaduct for us old timers): "Hope"— it was spray painted there before the water covered it, then went down and revealed it again—on what day did this become a losing battle? Answer: we didn't lose— it appears that over 1000 houses may be destroyed...
        —KXMC News

—I watch the blue scroll line stream across the screen as the camera pans across houses window and roof deep in water—

the streets are canals—the whole area is silent as a swamp—
the white print on the scroll reads, "Please control use of
water"—

—war-fight-struggle-battle-how many days did it rain before
the flood? 40? —that's what they told us when we looked at
the house we bought right by the river: you do not need flood
insurance—the story of Noah does not apply—People have
been washing their cars during this flood? Now? The car
washes were running?

—"...outwitted the river. It was a crap shoot; we just built
the dike, load for load—we almost feel guilty that we saved
this area—now we have 30 more families to help others"
            —KXMC News

—river still in flood—over 800 homes done for—how many
people to house, get back to work and school by this fall?
Then winter comes—

—(blue scroll across the screen) When I saw regular
programming it was "Lets Make a Deal", all those people
dressed like fools, yelling and shouting, and the ribbon on top
says, Boil Order Still On, Broadway Not Open—

—the shock of the flood wears off as the water recedes, and
those who have dry ground and those who lost their homes
to the water become aware-some want to go on; some
cannot; and the leadership seems to be evaporating—heroes
of the moment become robbers and bums before our eyes—
in other words like us—and now that the Broadway bridge is
open, the traffic is insane—everyone wants to go anywhere
they haven't gone—the water sits like a stagnant swamp on
the west end of town, you can see it from University Avenue,
in the center of old Minot—people are awake to the fact that

they do not have a home for the winter—businesses are going under—and the cry is, "Why is there no money for us?" I say, "Did you vote for tax money for disaster relief? No? Neither did anyone else." I am a cruel man—I am not Jesus, once again.

—If You Don't Stop Crying, You Can't Hear The Music:

I guess I mean, our boats are leaking and everyone's bailing, but our buckets have holes—big ones. And that reminds me of the little white enamel chamber pot my mom bought me (we had no indoor plumbing) when I was two, and she made me so proud of it. I suppose that's how she potty trained me. Smart move, Mom, but what a strange thing to be proud of.

Anyway I grew hollyhocks on the south side of the cow barn when I was a little older, and every day I would carry my now-leaking and not-needed chamber pot filled with water to the hollyhocks, but by the time I got there, even if I walked fast, only about half the water was left.

I suppose if I told that to my Dallas cousin he would tell me about the symbolism of a broken vessel and spilled water being a blessing. I told him about a dream I had a few years ago when dad was needing a lot of my care, and he said something like that.

In the dream I was pulling a little red wagon with an urn filled with water across a bumpy rocky hillside to get it into my brother's house and onto a shelf. With much difficulty I finally made it, although half spilled, but when lifting it to the shelf, I dropped the urn and it broke, spilling all the water. I crumbled to the floor sobbing, but became aware of these words: if you don't stop crying you can't hear the music. So I stopped crying and heard indescribably beautiful vocal harmonies, layers upon layers. And when I woke up my face was wet with tears, but for a while I could remember that music.

—E Mail (South of Mandan)

The Editor:

A man and woman I know well
Are plotting out the hillside down the
Road from me: a home,
A home they haven't built yet,
The home they lost a week or so ago
In the greatest flood we've seen—
We don't need an allegory for this tale—
This tale is allegory on the bone—

A doe and fawn I met today
Looked in through the window from my lawn
And then just ambled on across the
Yard and up the coulee in the trees,
After the flood that was the meanest flood we've seen—

Dragon Flies and Monarchs loop against
The tail wind of the only Northwest breeze we've had—
As displaced creatures of the valley
Slowly climb up hill to us,
And Grandma tries to keep her flowers
All alive with water from the flood,
Flowers that she moved here to the higher ground
To escape the widest river that we have ever seen—

All this is the allegory, the proverb we call mystery:
"The One Who Is" is not the one we thought;
I AM! Is not the thing we think,

Not the She-He-It we may have made—

Look beyond and see the glimmer and the gleam—
Glimpse the King and Queen of Heaven's wild domain—
The lesson is the river that will always rise again,
And the river of the Milky Way that we will always sail—

Editor's question to several people: What are the things you
hope to see after the flood?

—When the weight of the catastrophe really arrives and the
flood plain is covered with mud and junk, I hope to see
someone explain how this could have happened—

—A Monarch Butterfly—Dragon Flies feasting on
mosquitoes and drumming away in the air instead of a Black
Hawk—

—I want to hear something, not see it: the sound of a screen
door slapping the frame early in the morning, or at supper
time, or at sunset—

—I want to look out the window and see blue sky and hear
the bells of IST Pres or Little Flower—

—I want to see the lights over the valley from my house and
hear the tires droning on Broadway when I get up in the
middle of the night to get a drink of water—

—What about the first time I hear the rotors of a helicopter
or an emergency siren and I don't get sick to my stomach—

—I want to see water from the top of shower nozzle, or a
sink tap—

—I want to flush the toilet in my own house—

—brown river water in a slow moving channel, slow as cold
molasses, far down in its banks as I go for a walk in Oak Park
—I want that feeling I get when I can actually see the silence
of an early Sunday morning: that silence.

***

Sunday Matins: Lost Text

Hurricane Irene pounds the East Coast,
One fist of water, one fist of wind
These plains float in phoenix ash,
A mile high cloud of dust and
Drought so packed up above it
Looks as if you could walk it up to the moon

But this morning I am still here
In the last camp ground on the way to the sacred hill
The grass is lit with 10,000 diamonds
After a late night storm

In this far from perfectly beautiful world
I juggle the planet around in my head
Here in this light Sunday morning breeze
The birds ignore me with their songs

Not a single mosquito buzzes my space
Yet I still have this time to wrestle with gods
As I pause just between the sun and shade
To notice the smell of the human-
Bad tobacco smoke drifts to my nose
No one seems upwind of the smell

A catbird calls
I am not fooled
I know the fable,
The cat and the bird
Memory calls me
I weep and laugh these days,
Sometimes one and the same
I know enough to dry my eyes
Death is the tempting delusion
So I say, "Screw you"
I can see the door and gate
To the garden
Where guest and host
Walk in light
We are connected, you and I
Fear not, a voice says,
I will take you all along

***

"Why does this generation ask for a sign?
I tell you this:
No sign will be given this generation"

St Mark 8: 12-13

I say, "The sign of Jonah"
She says, "How is that a sign?"
Me again, "Fish belly Sunday sand dune puke up!"

Polly Anna Piously, girl of newborn bigotry
Waits to find her way to the inquisition,
A story only stoning, stakes and confession tell

Me, I, mine, I want to have no story

Lost in details, phenomenology of failure
I hum the tune, the only story I can tell,
I love…la, la, la, la, la, twill be my theme in glory…

She comes seeking solace she says,
In her Christian weeds and stress,
To "find her faith again"
She will see her job to break me
She seeks my secret—I can't say—
And works her will to break me

My job? To have no clue…
Unlike Job, I can't protest
My innocence is go-one,
Just my mother's Bible and
The broken, beaten, brain and song

Adventure? Phen…
Mystery? Menom…
Horror? Phenomen…
Heretical conspiracy?
PHENOMENOLGY
The hard forged quest that's left for me

God or Devil, details, touches, textures
A sweet, sweet yellow weeping onion
That my soul teeth peel—

     ***

Some Poet, said,
"…No one escapes,
Not even the man who believed he was chosen to do so,
For when the dark came down he cried out, 'Father, Father,
Why have you forsaken me?' To which no answer came"

Now poet, that's what you say or saw,
But the Man did not believe he would escape—
Unlike you or me or the deer in the head lights,
He believed to die. The answer was a rolling stone

Torn, stretched muscles, swollen tongue,
Ligaments ripped from Joseph's best joints,
Blinded, bloodied, light blistered eyes
The twitching fingers ruled by shot nerves
Severed by nails hammered in through the wrist
No pious painted sculpted gore is gore enough

Held beyond the stretch in gravities' pull,
Stillness, then motion, then pain,
Gravity, suffocation,
Came the answer he knew would come
From before the planet cooled to hold a life:
Blood mixed with water, then death

What can you see when you don't believe?

Ever stumble into a pitch-dark room
With your fingers wrapped around
An aluminum baseball bat?
Crouch down low, there in the dark
And pray until you can see…the dark

***

God blinks back tears

The robin born this spring flies into my plate glass window
I find it soaked and dead in the hailstorm
The second one since May

Their house burned down last year
This year, the flood took it almost to the day: it was
    complete
I live in a flooded city: 1 billion dollars is the cost

Senior citizens, fixed income families, university students
And a few people with money make up the loss

Contractors take up to 3 days to get a work permit

In the mean time, white butterflies fiddle around,
Barely cast shadows, chase and spiral in each
Other's slip stream and do not notice the problem at all
If you believe in heat index, today it will be 110 degrees

Seniors do ads for AARP: over 100 billion dollars for
SS and hospital care—someone is catching on.
Senator, congressman, how are things in the old
Swamps, drained, but remember mosquitoes and history:
    DC?

It is 97 degrees with 90% humidity— the flood zone
It smells like feedlots, lagoons and rotten luck

The peaches are drying up on the trees of Texas
Part of the great American desert needs a hurricane
The northern locations need fans, air conditioning
And three months of North Wind,

While the second largest earth filled dam in the world
Bulges and swells under the weight of the water,
Smashing out the penned up Missouri River—

So we have two river systems that never were

Supposed to flood: The Corpse of Engineers refuses to
Learn to blush at its misguided, arrogant science
And still looks good in businesslike camouflaged duds

***

At midnight, the windows are covered with mist
As if the river gave up on the frontal assault of the flood
And crept up out of its banks in a lighter, subtler way,
Allied itself with the air and then condensed on earth

This morning the overgrown rock garden across the
Street was a scene of constant war and strife
I swear cock robin picked the squirrel and drove him
To hiding, and all for no reason I can see

Next the robin went to digging, worms or grubs or show?
Then white butterflies in groups of two,
One group of two or many, how can two eyes know—?
Tortured the robin—he really was bothered and

Tried to ignore, knowing the pairs of aerial flutter
Heads could not be caught by beak or flight,
Or else they had the chemical mystery that made them
Taste like rotten, polluted things

The pretense didn't work a bit—the butterflies kept on
That robin as he worried the earth like a pervert near
The room where all the girls have gone to try on clothes
He hopped away from the weeds and hidden stones

Then he fluttered on Roberts Street
But the whites wouldn't leave him alone.
Another dead robin on the balcony this morning:
Two for this summer, a total of 12 or so in 13 years

The robins always seem to come in pairs
Do they live in essential loneliness after a window crash?
No information shared—no culture pooled between us:
The nest and egg, the birth, first flight, next year?

Nothing learned: plate glass walls in front of sky
Means no protection from the shock, the sudden smack
From nowhere and the broken neck in flight;
Lonely limits, lack of knowledge, death and then again

Do we want our Lord to step right in and fix this?
"No more plate glass; robins, wake up; know the sign of
        glass!"
Now the serpent was wily—you can hit the glass, you know;
You will not die—God wants the power of glass, kept it for
        herself

No, we meddle in the midst of God's own mystery trains
Of life, or death, and think we see, but know the glass is dark:
Grace note, mystery, coup de grace, a flock of strafing
Yellow finches buzz bombs the corpse in what seems like
        sheer delight

***

10 the pm late last night the heat index at 107, wet and hell
Then the early morning thunderstorm, imported from the
        south,
Now the wind, high northwester, skies as blue as oven fired
        glaze
The garbage truckers meet and greet out in our beat up street

Windows open, save the screens, let the cool winds blow

Clear the sticky rooms for light; wind's the way this prairie
    gets a name
The garbage boys are singing, shouting in the breeze as they
Pile dead branches in the truck, another day, and air that they
    can breathe

***

With my NPL/crypto Christian commie background, I ain't
    too optimistic—
I am still looking for justice for widows and orphans—
Any body seen the year of Jubilee lurking around the corner?
Uncle Sam and Lady Liberty gave Jubilee the slip at midnight
    on Wall Street
And we haven't been able to find her since! INRI?
Supply, demand, supply demand, the landlord's got the flood
    in hand!

***

All We Captives Hear

As the hysteric preacher prances
And bleats and honks beneath
The cross on the fake stonewall,
Crouches down, whip-waves his arms
And howls some feeble reasons
(Thus the volume: violence!)
Spits some spite into his wireless mike

I hear the still deep bass
And soprano duet
Of the wind in the eaves of the roof—-the boom
Of some unshackled soul

The keen from Sinai, Elijah, Shekhina,
And I pray that melody—
"Reach all the ears of this raving
Preacher's grief struck congregation,
So One Word is all we captives hear"

***

Gravitations

Two nights before the moon is full
It looks too full to me
Here in the needle eye of the valley wall
Wheat dust floats high in the sky
Flood dust hovers in the light
Raised up by 10,000 days of rush
And the combined chaff of 10,000 fields
Combines lined like armored columns
Two days after a battle
In the flooded city down below,
Red light, green light, flash and burn,
Red, orange, white/blue head lights,
Brake lights, sirens, beepers, diesel groans
The dusty dusk lies down beneath
The deeper, cleaner sky
The lights run ribbons—expectation,
That seductive promise, a Saturday night
But half the streets are flooded:
Crap, debris, old lost causes, downed-out dikes
Sand bag city sludge—the water is still not down

Here is the fact: there is nowhere left to go
That the water hasn't been
I go to bed when the moon is high
Up before dawn, the same moon hangs

Above the western bluff

Here is the thing: her gravity,
Something I call true love,
Keeps me on the curve
Even when we sleep
No matter where the water
Thunders in the night
Her pull tows me into this spot:
High ground

***

And It's Too Early To Sleep

On the spear of the moment
At the possible verge, the edge of the bed
Some great galloping revelation in
The minutia of probable problems caused by?
I am too tired to re-create the worlds

The late September afternoon
Lays light and rapture all across
The gold oak floor
Light blazes in the wind cut
Trees and splatters shadows,
Dancers on the gleaming wood

I am too tired to re-create the worlds

So let's take a walk
I need a walk
Accept the loss, the loose
But love forged bond we share,
The clay and dust on bone

With you alone
Who might not misunderstand?
I tried, continued, and will
Try the will, or fate or genes again,
To love this earth in
Tunes and words,
But now I'm tired
As Jesus' blood shot eyes.

Come walk; just stroll
These flooded prairie streets with me
September and the light is right
The street lights on
The dusk, near cloaked in dark
The dove wings whispered dark
And I don't want to sleep
I want long shadows,
Lovely under leaning trees,
And leaning, long lost light
And I do not want to lie down and sleep

***

Mid-Week Wastes

Oh this great, climactic Wednesday afternoon!
A car has hit this squirrel
And drags its grey body with front legs and paws,
Out of the grey street, this bright sunny street,
Rear legs useless, lagging behind, limp fur,
Muscles and bones are already dead-
"Boy in the front seat beside me,
Don't notice; don't see this, please—
You've already seen enough today,
13 and bruised by change and desires—

A long purgatory at school, a long drag"
Then we're in the garage
And safe in the house—you are home

Sick at heart, I look out a window
The rose bush next door
In mid-autumn bloom, maroon
Set off by the concrete walls
Can't wash the waste, the
Useless loss, the dragging tail
The taste of fur is on my tongue,
The bitter sour of mid-week, waste

***

Updike and Oil

"Oil money like a flash flood came and went…" —John
    Updike

Bone Town was never Tulsa, even before the Mouse River
    flood
And the "slow motion prairie Tsunami"[2]
Was never a flash, not at all,
More like a deluge where the ark waits for a dove
We needed Noah, an ark two by two
They sent us the a pop group, stage show and all,
That outfit, "The Black Eyed Peas"

Now Halliburton has settled right
Students and ancient survivors
Left from The Great Depression can't find a place to pay the
    rent

---

[2] Alfonse Koningsman, Dramaturgist

The water is gone
The guard is gone
The levee is bulldozed
The ghosts of the great flood linger in windowless, gutted
    buildings
And empty, deserted streets—without the street lights the
Darkness runs like oil down the sidewalks and weedy lawns
Water, air, oil and money run through fingerless hands

***

Down in The Flood

The Iraq Veteran falls asleep, passes out as he orders at the
    Drive Through—
The drive through worker 911's—
The Border guards respond—
They surround the Bagdad car, guns drawn—
When the veteran doesn't move, or
Responds to no demands,
They do a full assault—
The music in the veteran's car says
"God Only Knows Where I'd Be Without You"—
It rained 2 inches late last night
The whole town smells like fish—
A 911 celebration
People know what those three numbers mean;
If they ever did;
People know what those three numbers cost:
Like the Police sing, "Unpaid bills, Afghanistan hills"[3]

***

---

[3] The Police, "Bombs Away"

Autumn: Blue Jay Dedications

Nothing like the adrenaline shot
That jolts from the throat straight
Down to the gut
When the big blue jay,
Shell and peanut in his beak,
Lets loose with that blue shriek-
One high note in my sunrise eyes
It's a giant jerk of joy
On the balcony rail
In the great sweet light,
Autumn, Saturday,
Dedicate this time,
You get few hours
Outside the natter
Of the work day week:

Here, the last dry summer wind
Here, the house we clean to
Make our nest seem clear
Here to the southern light
That follows us through
The string of rooms we clean,
And finally night,
Some wine, a meal
And the sound of
The jay still down in my ears
Some angels are blue
And they don't sing hallelujah,
They shriek at the shock, Our Lord

***

God's Silence

—My love she speaks with silence, without ideas of violence
   —Bob Dylan

Just the next day, in some other kind of church
Where some of us had seen the angels fly above the flood,
Where the saints among us blend in with the
Bonetown, boomtown losers,
We baptized babies in the radiance
Of sunlit, stained glass light

His father holds him headfirst
Above the dark walnut font
As the water splashes down his head
The baby claps his hands
Upright again in his godmother's hands
While the pastor makes the sign of the cross
On the space just above his eyes
He reaches out and grasps the
Fingers that move across his face
When they light his candles
His eyes pop wide and wild;
Black holes absorb the light from stars
You can trade all wisdom you hear
To know the nothing just one baby grasps
In his grip the Great I Am is known

***

Motion of Love Through Still Life

It could be a still life
But we are not still at all,
Unless you count "still here"

The red-aired haze paints a late in
October Saturday afternoon
Your chicken sizzles in Barbeque
Sauce on the smoking grill,
Perfumes the air of the space
Back here between woodshed
And pine fence on three sides.

The dried Scots pine cones and needles
Are piled in a perfect red brown
Blanket across the patio bricks
And heaped on the green metal table and chairs
The half empty bottle of Sauvignon Blanc
Picks up a green tint from the table
And then a red tint from the air,
So calling it white wine wouldn't be right
The wine is cheap but tastes of
The dry air, smoke, and pine,
A last light in the darkening day
But you and I sit, clearly aware of
The fire that burns in our chests
It's o.k. if this still life breaks, dissolves and is gone.
We make the moment, an ache of joy,
The motion of love through a still life
And into our own deep time
Lust for more, even more,
And eternity moves beneath the speed of light.

***

Between Finite and Infinite, part III

Biography of a Companion

I did what I thought I should do all week long. On a warm
    day, three cold mornings,
October dumped heavy leaves into the holes in the ground
    until they were piles. It was wet one day, dry for three.

I listened, taught, prayed; I even sang old Beatles songs.

But today I will sit; it was all: wrong. So I hear the Word,
    watch his life float by on a video screen and wonder. In
    some photos there is no smile, but a look of pensive
    wisdom that says, "I do know; I do."

The old hymns at the funeral are somber, not sweet, and too
    true. He did have those oddball grins.

But today, we are taught to visit the sick, to pray for the
    dying; we bless the defeated;
We prepare the bodies of the dead; we eat tasteless ashes of
    grief; only dill pickles at the afternoon lunch could give
    this sorrow flavor.

Sunday afternoon, wind, low Sun, wind, low Sun, and you
    review all the stories you know. He stands by the
    window and looks over your shoulder. The lopsided
    smile is real.

When he moved away to the desert mountains, he already
    knew he was deeply loved: Beatitudes, retold by him…

***

Redemption

If you hide your sorrow just enough,
Yet let the rain and wet leaves show,

Somewhere in the world,
Carried on the water and the wood,
A sister, brother weeps with you
And carries you along
The road to limited joy
Redemption ain't a preacher word
Redemption is a time, a touch, a place
In the fields of Albion-
Jerusalem, a blessed, loving face

***

After the Flood and In The Boom

"I swear I pulled out across Broadway right on the green light
—

This demonic roughneck in a Tobey Keith special with
Arkansas plates comes like a wind on an oil slick street
Across the lane and behind me, into the right lane, comes up
    on
One of those giant, slipstreams—to suck me into his wake,
So I gun my gentle Honda van and jump into the lane in
    front of him
In the hopes of making my next right turn,
And I hear engine thunder and diesel perfume on the wind
As he tears by and leaves me in his own jet stream,
A leer on his face, he drop kicks by.

I say, Hey, where's the cops when these lunatic outlaws
Make the sonic blast out on Broadway, with the kids on their
    way to school?
And then I see a cop on the corner, out of his car,
Watching the sunrise while the Oil Boom blasts past,
And I think, Well, I should call the Chief of Police,
And I'm thinking it still, indignant citizen that I am,

There on my way home from the drop off at school,
Come to a stop for my right turn on 6th Street to
Head back north, and who pulls out right in front of me?
The Chief of Police himself, with never a nod or even a how
    do you do."

***

The Shrine of Three Mary's

That black cat was just a kitty last summer
And chased the monarch butterflies up and
Over the hill to the west,
The cat so small the tall grass moved in waves,
The waves the way to follow its flashy leaps

Over the hill, when the cat comes down this spring,
The kitten is all but gone
A new motel is soon to grow from
A power point plan on the planning commissar's wall,
Up the sky line and into the earth
Who are all these sleepy people,
These travelers coming in off the roads,
To stay here in Bonetown now?

A doe, a song in a brown blur of fur
Runs east, up the hill
Past the airport and out into the fields

"Sometimes I dream of other minutes
By hidden memory retold…" –Pushkin, "Eugene Onegin",
    Vlad. Nabokov trans.

In this dream I remember to call out to the shrine of Three
    Mary's

On the bluff above the hills:
Magdalena in the red scarf, Wisdom's old whore,
Mary the student who studied at Jesus feet
And anointed the same feet and head as well,
Who wrapped and unwrapped her own brother,
For and from the grave;
Mary the Mother of our Lord
As she pondered in sorrow
The swaddling clothes,
The shepherds, astrologers, sheep
And then, her service to gott, a raven of sorrow,
From the foot of the cross
And on to the shadowy garden of tombs—
The empty tomb—Mark says, "They were afraid"

Lift the gravestone off my eyes
Let me free all the love of my years
Into one eternal move,
Into the form of the brown, blurred, running doe

***

Works of Mercy

The two does graze on the steep
Slope of our dandy lion lawn
In the clear, green stained broad
Evening light after two days of rain—
Then is the first time we hear
(In fact I hear them right now)
The mourning doves since fall,
And right through the glass—
It is still too cold out to open the window—
Sunday morning can be an untouchable
Ache filled with blue—

It can suck the gold right out of the sun—
Then the doves coo call again—
These acts of nature are works of mercy,
Are done with deep grace, the sweet mix,
Humility, pride in the fact of the Kingdom
Of God comes back—
The songs of nature, each new, unrepeatable,
And the sun's magnificent study of light
In the ancient of days, call her Grace,
And all this happens in one particular eye
Against the screen of neutral, life bearing sky—
Mary, Mary, Mary, where are we going to?

***

The stupendous wind blows in to blast the heat and humidity
    down
Roof joists creak and crack in memory of white winter storms
So the sky seems strange, no dust blowing, sure no snow in
    the air,
And it mirrors the sunlight in an eye-blinding prairie blue,
    blue, blue

Sparrows zip and swing, staying close to the ground, whipped
    in clouds
As the two Morning Doves give up cooing and tender old
    folks chat
To let their big breasted bodies off the of wires and soar on
    wings
That are used to dignity but in fact can outdo the robins and
    black birds

Who seem pretty cautious now that the wind is clear and
    fresh in July

The White and Yellow butterfly troops are battened down
   somewhere
And petunias in planters, daisies in beds are bent over
   sideways and
Just hang on by their roots in the planters and flowerbeds
   along the walls

Wind gusts up high and makes the trees wave in unison
   motion choirs
Down close to the earth the grass bends over, leans to the
   east so it
Looks like some huge old massive invisible thing has laid it
   flat, a
Flooding river of wind, in fact, is determined to do just that

Thus comes Clark the Dog, dragged his rented human walker
   by her
Leash; a solid girl, the dragged along by the black prancing
   curly haired mutt
Who jumps, bounces, struts, tries to run and wants to take a
   leak or
Two on every moving stand of tall grass, bush or stump he
   sees

He gives the day his delight and dash; wind in the tall grass is
   joy
A good long piddle declares the day one that any fool of a
   dog can
See is made by the maker of days: God-but dog? Dog of
   God who
Tells this world just how much simple mystery heaven's wind
   will allow

***

—Oh Lord, whatever I have said in this book that comes of thy prompting, may thy people recognize it; for what I have said that comes only of myself, I ask of thee and of they people pardon.   —St. Augustine, "De Trin." XV, 28

I often write words from my vision as though
God's finger points like a gun at my head,
As if the dead lines dance, truth or justice or money involved
Onto the note card in through the eyes or ears,
Process, click, click, snap it—focus the lenses and get it down
     before…?
The only Deadline is death—and I am not sure of that

***

Clouds of robins and sparrows sparring in the purple leaves
     of the Canadian Cherry, Cloud of dragon flies, little gold
     dive bombs, huge blue high hummers,
Working the mosquito farms over the low wet ground after
     the rain, a crowd of Black birds ratchets the air and rake
     the lawn beneath the ash trees and me here
With the cloud in my head—wake me up friend creatures—

I am not Snow White,
But I am on to what you are doing
And want to help, work creation
Around to the point where
Omega means new eternal ranges of sight:
Last night, the Milky Way touched down!

***

Three sparrows in the old wood tub which the former
     owners left when they

Abandoned shore for ship and shipped and skipped out like a
    flung flat stone
Across the mystic Puget Sound, sailed that ship, "Small Rain"
    away, a
Folk song on the mist of legend memory and fate: three
    sparrows fly, turn
Into five, launched from the tub, and shock the pansies—
Volunteers again this
Year as the petunias
Droop and sigh,
Too much racket,
Magic birds, too much or little rain
Small Rain sails out of the Sound
I hear sails
Stiffen in the wind

***

Just where is it written, this eternal tempest in the teapot
    apocalypse of being?
All this, "Was it, is it will be evermore?" Buy THAT at some
    super store!
Let us seek out heaven with the wisdom of the wise, two year
    olds and fools
Who's that little guy out by the weedy rock bed on his own?
Sparrow's body, brown to black and bright red finch's stolen
    head,
He searched god in grass like a praying, red alerted martial
    monk.
So find him in some bird book, and if we do, like they say,
    those book believers,
Promise me, we'll find god's word for word right in the text:
    literal, inspired—
I have lost god in the works, transpirations, old translations,
    paraphrases,

And contorted Lit. Crypt method of Tradition Hysteria and
   sub text, ala the Anguish Departments of the world—the
   is more of God in a chemistry lab—

God found me with my head attached, my body all but meat,
   and threw me in the
Water where I knelt upon the mountain stones beneath the
   water, and down there deep, beneath my knees, below the
   stones, I heard the word, I heard, and know enough to
   stop right here and say no more—I will lean on Billy
   Blake again!

***

The robins and sparrows back from who knows where,
   before my eyes, outside the
Windows are tearing up the berries in the branches of the
   cherry, though the berries
Are still green to me—the leaves are purple-black-the juice is
   in the roots already
Ready for the winter in the secret sessions of root planning
   for the cold just as the
Robins and sparrows all act wild, drunk and goofy—they
   make a burlesque matinee
Mad matins, vocal, yokel vespers—I'll find comfort in the
   memory on my midnight
Maniac, yearning –from the weakness of my weakest
   afternoon to the local hell of
Sleeplessness when I crave the whimsy that will sweep close
   to heaven's joke

***

We pull into the parking lot of the local grocery this hot and
   soggy afternoon.

On the window of an SUV we see a stenciled ribbon, pink, a
    slogan,
"Save The Ta Ta's", while a man, some good years old, and a
    boy of 13 gape.
Then the man says "What is that supposed to mean?" and, "I
    don't get it at all." The 13 year old gives off silence in the
    blush of empty space——

Now me, a pesky pervert since primary grades in vice, and
    these two women, Upright, serene in place and time, we
    who know the "Ta Ta" slang, we snort and Giggle like
    old lover's of the bride at the wedding when she makes
    the vows she broke when we were kids. "What's so
    funny?"—Giggle, snort— and at that moment I see
    Christopher and Pooh bear in that scene, out on the
    bridge, at the end of the tale and think of all the little kids
    who know the other meaning, " Ta! Ta! Oh, Farewell—
    stiff upper lip in sorrow and all that!"

As my dirty brain goes Ta Ta' ing around the golden calf, a
    cow, the girls of Play Boy 1964, the she wolf suckles
    Roman Twins of Empire, all the brew, ha! ha! and
Milking stools—National Geographic girls, and me? See I've
    mythologized the very glands that give a baby mammal
    life, idealized and; idolize, sex up, and ruin on the rack of
    store bought push and lift and separate—I will not be the
    old man we see, all sneeze and squeeze and stare and gape
    and make the stupid jokes—

Sometimes I do like to sit and maybe "…just do nothing"—

"Oh, Farewell now, my Mother's milk—you're a show girl
    now—but the truth of god's own truth is that we're
    mostly suckled, young or old, if we are loved, like any
    monkey, kitty cat or calf—what a twisted gift, to make the

flesh that gives us milk into a messed up, sexy, sometimes
nasty word.

Part II:

T.S. Eliot In Bonetown, Dakota, After the Flood

"A breath of pine, and the wood song fog
By this grace dissolved in Place" – T.S. Eliot, Marina

The snow of three days dissolved last night
And in the full light, Saturday,
The smallest sparrows,
Bonetown big in sparrow terms,
Were fierce and loud in the cherry trees
Beneath the half moon
That will be done by Christmas

White sky, grey, the frost on the roofs, cars and trees
Dissolve from echo to silence, half formed prayers
The sun breaks gold to rise against
The flat, still sea of blind blue sky
This one-week before Christmas,
5 months after the flood,

" And by this grace" the pain and hope
"Dissolved" until the dark water dreams were done
And our feet touched solid ground again, this "place".

***

Snow Again Tonight

The snow fell all night
we were forced to sit and learn

and eat and be eaten by silence,
a communion of warm blood
the sun barely came up
here come the dogs
and bosses' plows
Why does someone
always piss in the snow?
Hope it snows again tonight

***

The Winter Abandoned in Feathers: Dreams

The January afternoon looks like it will go down cold with a
    twist of lemon ice-
Sunset manages its drunken Nordic depressive promise for
    the present-
The wind comes up and blows light powdered makeup over
    the roughed up,
Thawed and then frozen old, blackened, browned and dog
    pissed snow-
The full moon is so bright that the streetlights seem dim
    down in the valley,
And the white all around takes on the holy dead bones tone
    of the saint-
The few streaks of clouds between the stars and the earth are
    slashed scraps-
A light, high, wind-blown power makes me want to step
    outside naked,
Just say forget it until my feet stick to the ground, and I am a
    tall pole-

In the dream that night I walk with two friends, men, one still
    living, and one

93

Dead for years, both at home on the streets of this town as
    they can be-
They lead me to a place west on the railroad tracks near the
    river,
And we are all a bit sweaty because it is suddenly early
    summer—my eyes are a
Green touched with yellow light, so kind to my vision—after
    January -

The two men leave, and then there you are with me, you and
    me again, and we
Are standing on a sandy dirt road in tall green grass up to our
    knees-
We are silent, and we look at a small barn flanked by an even
    smaller house-
The paint is all gone, and the windows are broken, but you
    could tell that the
Structures are solid, ready to be cleaned up and lived in again-
We walk on a rock path on the west side of the house and
    barn and find a giant
Twisted cottonwood in a small clump of chokecherries and
    Chinese elms-
We follow the path into the brush—it narrows—we push
    new growth out of
Our way and find ourselves next to the trunk of the single
    cottonwood-

It is mangled, lightning struck, branches snapped from the
    weight of snow
And the blasts of the wind—there are nests full of feathers in
    many branches,
Straw and twigs and fluffy white feathers—most of the nests
    are empty,
But there is one huge white bird in a nest about 30 feet
    above,

Out on a large branch—it is watching us, unafraid, even looks
   a little bored—
The ground around the tree is neither rocky nor sandy,
But packed as hard as baked clay or an adobe floor.
There is no grass, twigs or debris to trip up the feet or clutter
   the sight-
There are no scraps of paper in the brush, not one bag in the
   tree, and the
Silence is as deep, an empty church early on a Saturday
   morning—

I look in your eyes, and you show no interest, in me or in this
   place, just as I realize that I think this place is perfect, that
   we should buy it immediately
And live in it—you do not speak, as usual when you have no
   clear words—
There is every chance to take here, and I have no desire to
   ask or explain-
Among the cottonwood roots, on the packed clay floor, the
   shadow and light
Around us, I see that you are flying, alive inside, or on you're
   way to that
Someplace I finally have no chance to go, no hope to see—
   instead I see the
Bird, huge and calm in the nest; I am bathed in the shadows,
   and feathers fall around me, on my head, on my
   shoulders—

When did we become a question of crossing gaps, a word of
   distance?

***

These Things I Scribble Are Acts of Prayer

God always talks back to me…Concrete image
(See the words above)

I do not listen

Do not like what I do hear

Am too afraid to listen

Am too brave to listen

Too full of fury to just listen

Nature sends me—big mixed message

God: the last refuge of scoundrels like me

You do not listen

Do not like what you do hear

Too afraid to listen

Way too brave to listen

Too full of your God to listen

Nature sends you: big mixed message

God: the last refuge of a scoundrel; you are one of them

21st Century Digital Beings, we are too full of science,

Digital pixel wax in our ears,

She who has ears then let him hear

***

From February, 2011, In The Woman's Calendar:
"Wake up ladies—your time is here!"

***

I Have To Tell

...Of the black cat before sunrise. It dashed across my eyes
and across the street below in the sound break of a barking
dog. Then the black cat appeared like even it was surprised,
an impossible distance from behind the yellow house, as if it
had passed through matter and did not know how it
happened—the Black Pearl, the Flying Dutchman of a
leaning waning moon danced, disappeared, appeared again,
firing broadsides of white light into the clouds. Down in the
street, the black cat met itself, sniffed it and we discovered
there were two. This story is the heart of why we need to
trust flesh of the people around us, leave the flesh of the
animals alone, and know that there is a bread of moonlight
that will last forever. I saw it with these broken eyes. Believe
me so I can live with both of us.

***

The Whole Deal

A tree was the first mystery,
How to get into the tree,
How to get out once you get in,

How to walk on two legs and
Lose a tail with a tale of an apple spliced in—
Death was the second mystery
(Now who spoke those words, old Kibbler?)

Sheepherder bashed
By homicidal, insecure famers—

Over east there where people drawn their words on paper
    with ink,
The whole deal became a matter of style, cunning and sudden
    death—
Over west, the whole deal became a matter of matter,
And as a result, we are now running out of time,
Painting words on paper made of waste from dead trees
And eating the earth as a form of weird entertainment

According to the Norse, Lakota and Christians,
A tree will provide the solution the final deal

***

The Last, So Take the Time
(For Red Watson)

Sleep in the perfected angle of full moonlight on a Saturday
    night in February
When cream runs through the tall and gleaming windows
Almost doze in a sun flooded heat of a Sunday afternoon
    when the sounds of the house builders hammers and
    saws smack against the long whistle calls of 100 years of
    steam and diesel powered freights on the distant thunder
    of the tracks

While a flock of giant sparrows do a windy choral jazz call,
dance and response to the Southeast wind blowing in the
three evergreens down the street

The war is over; the traumatic weekends of Windsor ditches
and wild nights of insomniac madness are far in the past
—nostalgia, impossible and real are all we can feel, and
we can lie here forever with a magazine or a Bible on one
knee and know that this is the last time to take the time,
the place beyond all place, the light of moon, sun,
remembered sounds, know that time is there for taking,
memory there for all healing, so take the time and mold it,
the stings of moon and sun, until it lifts out of sleep,
dreams, hope and death, until you lift into the revealed
home: at last, the place we find what we knew God knew
before the multiverse was born.

***

New Yorker: Testimony on The Big Reveal
3/5/12

First the Geese flew over, 6 flights
Two days before St. Patrick's Day
Then I heard the flute—
There was no music in the house

And I fell into the dream

An Excursus and interlude:

On Dunn's "Testimony" and Adam Gopnik's review, "The
Big Reveal", of Elaine Pagels book, "Revelations:
Visions, Prophecy, and Politics in the Book of
Revelation"

Stephen Dunn, not John Donne, and Adam not-with-Eve
   Gopnik
Got the gist with Pagels (Elaine), the Gnostic resurrector—
Stephen woke up in the middle of night in the middle of
   Revelation,
And met the "Lord", divine communication, wisdom and
   beyond,
Stephan, not the martyr, but Dunn "...man like Christ, not a
   big ole hog"
Gopnik read Pagels in the realms of Beasts and Bloody
   Lambs and Whores,
Pagels awash in the private wisdom of her Gnostic
   excavations

Here's my testimony on this Big Reveal— Stephan, St John,
   Adam,
Pagels— from the Lord in the middle of the morning light:
St. Paul's dates by all respected erudition are nearly 50 years
Before the Patmos bard broke dates for a "Whore of Baby
   Boom"—
Jesus preached the Kingdom; the church still preaches Jesus
   the Christ,
Ala Paul, who fought the merde of disemboweled Gnostic
   visions,
And in fact, Paul was a Jew, proud of the faith he knew,
That "Pharisee of Pharisees'" becomes the fool
For Christ (in Corinth, Pagels, Corinth)—
And always Paul remained the cross arms that connected—
The "Jews demand signs, and the Greeks demand Wisdom"

So is this, "The histories of faiths are all essentially the same,
A vague and ambiguous, millennial doctrine..." new old
   Adam?

Gopnik, not with Eve? Are you just one journalist? Are you a
   prophet, too?
Have you not read the Bible, or the many books the Bible
   made?
Who reads the good book outside tradition/history/lit?
   Crit./source work/
Sitz em leben, sitz in book? Journalists, Gnostics,
   fundamentalists, I see,
And by the way, no Bishop buried Sappho or the Gnostics in
   the waddi
In the desert where Elaine could find in the cave or in a tree
   —

It was the Gnostics buried, hid their own wisdom in rock and
   sand,
Because they didn't want the fleshy church folk's in the know,
   so...

The flute was playing
I spoke to old Heisenberg,
And he said; never look too close at the things you see
The microscope moves
The telescope jumps
The Lab Coats see what they often wish to see

The flute was playing
I heard Einstein sing,
"Eeeeeeeeeee, equals MC^2
The cosmos moves at the speed of light
Don't you let the
Black holes make you scared!"

And then The Cracked Pot Prophet spoke from beneath my
   gut:
"Out of the black holes comes the Revelation
We rise in a new earth, fresh blood from the womb,

Wet with the blood of the mother of God!"

***

Good Friday Vespers

Come ewe who lamb your wool heavy load
Burdened down by the lists, the stupid human
Nasty phrases used in the ugly stillbirth
Process, selfish sole-fistic justice—
For Judgment or Sentence,
Join me beneath the altar rail,
Beneath the cross in the old stucco
Church at midnight

We need no more blood and thunder!
Absolution, dissolve away these
Private, petty, self-possessing sins.
Empty the treasury box of pain.
If we are not here, this one holy night,
We have no business to be here at all
So, what will it take?

We are the church, a nation, a notion,
A race of freaks turned saint,
Half sheep, some half goat,
All angels disguised as beasts

***

Full Moon on Good Friday

1

In the fog at midmorning, midtown Bonetown,

On Third Street and Central Avenue,
We crossed the viaduct in holy parade,
This Saturday, St. Patrick's

Strange folks in shades and togs and
Oddball combinations—all of them green,
6 braided men from the New Town
Out to celebrate someone's birthday,
And us moms and dads and kids along,
Walking our winter-wasted bikes
To the cyclery for some air:
Resurrection not resuscitation!

There on Central we broke up and went our three ways,
Ebenezer's Pub, to Arnie's Bar and Val's Cyclery,
Three tribes on separate liturgical expeditions—

But be aware you greedy town,
You banker's realtors, you supply and demanders:
You have nothing to teach us,
And so we learned it all—and will, again, the hard way
But for a moment up on the bridge,
All the tribes were a union, communion,
The body and blood of the dream
Look out, for one day we tribes may all be one,
And not accidentally, for the purpose of
Hunting your dark dreams down—

And all this in the fog on St Patrick's Day,
Before the bells of St Leo's struck noon.

2

Third Wednesday of Lent

Outside the grocery store at dusk
Notice the sky isn't black—it's purple,
Thick snowflakes, wafers of water and ice
Later, back home, a candle burns, yellow-orange
Outside the hill to the west is black
But the streetlight makes a cone of orange in the snow
The black cat runs into the cone, turns gold
The silent room turns dark, then flickers yellow
Light strikes the wood floors,
The ice in a glass, while the past
Eight hours still chatter deep in the bones of the ears
Early this morning the light beat down against the black hill
The nearly full moon dumped white on the streets,
Drowned the glow of weak street lamps
The brown patchy lawns
Flooded white against the laws of gravitation,
All around the drowned town

There will be a full moon on Good Friday this year—

3

The Tulips

Our robins are back,
Here in the yard they seem to own-
Saturday morning looks like rain
The tulips are up,
But it's your two lips,
All two lips like tulips,
Seem to blossom this morning,
Absolutely impossible pink-
Your two lips are sleeping-
My two lips are mouthing this
Song beside you in bed-

I am tired, awake too early-
This last day of the week,
Limbs are soggy,
My head a ragged bush-
The leaves on the bark
On the branch of the
Book of my trunk
Are cold—your lips are budding
These days before
The psalms I sing
Are the psalms they sang
For a 1000 years-
The weeks before Holy Week
Good Friday looms-
The forecast is good-
Tulips open below the trees
To take the tree
That holds early fruit
From winter's pagan tomb-
Tulips, you must open-

There's moonlight this early,
Headed for full,
The sky still too high
Above these southern windows
The roofs, the trees,
April's fools are ready: now

4

Moon Psalms

Near, full moon, SW above
The house just after daylight
One crow is out—scout and crier too

105

The wind gusts up, and then lets up
Objects in the street grow clearer with the light
The kitten that we watched last year
Is grown and howls a yearning
Lovesick black cat blues
The crow caws back in a black old song
The full moon rise is still some time away
How many Passovers would it take
To make it up to Jerusalem
The temple made of stone is never really built
The temple made with hymns of flesh
Hides the God the poets all can see

5

The full moon, you heard me say, then turned this way,
Is forecast for Good Friday
Darkness falls at 9 pm this Day Light Savings Time
A pale white light grows out in the east
The stars are out, and above this house of prayers,
Saturn and Venus look like perfect signs
Then one star moves: the others watch
A jet, I know, breaks the still life of the stars
The geese are higher up above,
Crying their love songs in the colder dark

6

2 pm on any Tuesday, shortly after we ditch old frozen
     March,
Seems as warm and clear as the first spring morning
After the end of school
And through an open balcony door,
We hear the builders hammering, the saw whines in the wind,
Blue white sky, the sharp aired breeze

And my memory winds back to the ancient "Spot"
The un-mowed late May lawn
By the bright white house with the deep red trim—
So simple—2012 back to 1961-
I hear you car pull in the drive,
And a surge of powers shouts from in this thing
I seem to have to call my soul,
Deep in my diaphragm, down in my groin,
All the momentary wonder of your presence
Becomes the phenomenon of love

Grandma is out in the moonlight,
Digging the holes to plant potatoes
A long time before Good Friday
She is old, and she is slow,
And she says, with deeper eyes,
I know; softy then, again, I know

7

I have hated the parts that I can't make fit
Because there is no whole
The compartments break my spine
And the God within me dies
Stretch me out in 4 directions,
God to woman, child to sweet guitar
You would scream and run
As far as your could
Just from the goblins that you saw
Rise up from my chest

I found a nail as long as my true love's
Forearm today
For which we cannot picture a use
Jesus was so self-contained

In Wisdom Mother Son of Man,
All creation, water, cosmos, earth and air,
That he stayed put upon the cross
And would have without the nails he made
From love,
That he stayed put inside the tomb
For death,
Until the stone he made unmade itself
And rolled the hole away

8

I strike, but only glancing blows
My hard head splinters God's own rock
I bend the nails when I strike
People, do not be afraid
People you should be afraid
You have everything to fear with me
You and I all know we hate these holy words:
"Was it not needed that The Savior
Suffer all these many things?
(ouchi tauta edei pathein tou Christou)"

That little Greek word, e, d, e, and i: edei

9

I got up last night, Good Friday, at 3 am,
Come to pierce my sodden soul,
I had to see the moon,
I did, right there just above the trees,
A sky free of clouds, almost exploding
With full deep light
You see, as any child would say,
We need the moon, the little light

The moon does not need us
After today and Saturday,
Jesus has all the goods

10

Forecast and Foretaste

As the full moon was rising
After the rain,
And the wind had risen
To a tree whipped gale,
Two does stepped
Out across the paved street
And worked their way, gazing,
Grazing, alert, at 2 am
Do we need to know our
Mary's name in order for her to do the work?
Woman, wisdom, Mary, doe,
Nuzzle, beware and quietly
Work the rain and moon in time

11

We were driving down the street
She sees an 8-inch nail
So I jump out and grab it
The thing is thick enough
To pierce both ankles to a cross,
Even if the anklebones are thick

The wind came up Good Friday
The clouds began to move
Thunderstorms were forecast,
And Saturday it's snow,

So we're under the shroud
But not in Turin, once again
Sunday we'll be hunting Easter eggs
And tulips on white lawns

12

Full Moon Easter Ballad

First thing on Easter Morning,
Still full moon in rising sun,
The black cat chased two turkey hens
And had them on the run
Across the road and up the hillside
Where the standing stones
Turned rosy in the light
The Pheasant Cock was
Cracking wise as old men will,
Talking back to all the crows
Then the dogs were barking
In the valley down below
Where in churches people sang,
And some clung to the songs,
While up here the sky turned gold
The standing stones were white
There's honey in the whole
There's mystery in the garden,
Honey in the grave hole, child,
Holy sweet sting of death down in the hole,
But the joke will be on us
When the whole universe arrives
And wakes up full of joyful noise
And the angels bend the angles
Into curves to play the sweet
Blue beats on their drums and tambourines

13

Sun Tree Table Wind

The sun on Easter Monday
Someway finds a space between
The hills above the walls
East of this house, so its light
Can manage, spread through
Branches of Scots pine
On the grass outside the fence
That conceals the little nook-
Branches spread such patterns
As they become the filtered
Light that blows straight into
The kitchen where I stand and
Toss the dishes in the sink-
That filtered light strikes in
Yellow, golden, varnished soul,
Surface, table, counters,
Empty now but ready for a feast—
The surface of the table, still the
Size of the door it was,
Becomes the canvas for the
Sunlight brush to paint:
Newspaper, print and varnished grain-
Then light shifts because
The branches of the pine
Are floating on a subtle little wind
Now the branches turn from brushes
Into stenciled silhouettes,
And the table seems in motion,
Seems to lift up on light wings-
In Emmaus they saw victory,

The creator broke creation in
The tearing of the bread
And it all is very simple if
You simply stop to notice
Wood grain on the tabletop-

There is silence in the room right now-
It is a complex mystery too-
Only a physicist or five years old
Might tell me they can show me
Here a picture of the Holy Spirit then
On this table now-

"You are not the first person to reduce faith to a matter of
    touch."
—V. Nabokov

I am not the final person to tender faith
Like eye ball visions beyond facts.
Facts are what a human hand can touch.

Sun, earth move—fingers feel it,
In the eyes the variations,
In the movements of the light,
Where the table, once a tree, is now a
Shining vision screen-
This world around me slides away-
I stand up and stagger back,
Burned by the spirit in the sun splashed wood,
Burned to my heart with childlike fear
By the sun, tree, wind and light
As it merges, miracle on wood-
God will sit right here—hold on
Some one bring me something strong to drink-
Time to break this loaf of bread-

I stumble under weighted stories of
This thing called Easter, now,
As if I came with Cyrene and had to bear a cross
Beneath the shadow of the lash-
The leer upon the face of that hill,
For us, death in grace and faith,
Creates a destination, "Resurrection
And Redemption", reunion with
The source of life in every single thing-
We have never sought to learn or love
From deep in the black hole-
We escape and know we're blind-
If I had Mary Magdalene to comfort me right now,
Or even Thomas, "Come and touch me!"
I don't need to understand it Thomas-
Let me touch it! Let me hold it in my arms.
But no; 2000 years or so,
The shock of recognition,
Fearful death and resurrection
Has become my pious feeling,
Theology and careful thoughts-
You do not think it through,
And then write careful systems
On rebirth, the multiverse.
You reel in shock and horror,
And then fear, until the joy.
Terror is the word today-
Terror is the word to know:
What we will feel in the grip
Of daily death until we're shocked back into life

***

What My Mother Called Real Faith

At 9 am, the smell of beach, dead fish,
And the ocean comes through the open front door
It is 1500 miles to salt water in three directions
Head south and you'll end up in Terra del Fuego
Before you see the salt
So this smell comes from the rain,
From the steadily raining sky last night,
From my body,
My steadily seeping, sweaty meat,
And from the ancient sea that covered
This lost colony before the
River People escaped
Through a hollow log from the other earth
During that great mythic flood
And made this place dry land

To see what I mean, think this:
Futures are hidden in ancestor bones
And the grace of a God we have never seen,
A despised refugee on a cross—
What my mother called real faith

My Mother Conceived a What?

Choose to call them hard-forged truths:
Adopted clichés that
Were titles for observations,
Which always leads me back
To figure experience out for myself

Two pigeons, pompous and safe
On the overhang above the door
Of the Bagel Stop,

One silvery grey and white,
One deep purple and charcoal dust-
One hops on the other's back,
Attempts to make love
And falls off to the side like a drunk-
The other hops on the back of the
Clumsy oaf and coos and woos away,
But she/he/it just slips off too

The tom turkey struts like
The power drunk tyrants all do,
Surrounded by his harem
Dunned down in black and gray
When the garbage truck
Roars up the street from the east,
His wise women scatter
While he brandishes tail and wing in panic
And almost gets hit by the monstrous thing

Three doves in the apple tree,
Ornamental as the fruit the tree grows
Sudden eruption in combat-
One dove swoops,
Wing boxes another-
The third dove watches, quite still
When the aerial combat is over
And one dove escapes, alone,
The silent dove waits for the
Winner to land on a branch
And then flutters down-
Side by side they coo on honeymoon limbs of spring

When I was 40 my mother told me
That I was lucky to lose what I had never owned
And be found by the grace that

Chose to marry and take me on:
Birds of a feather, my mother said

My Mother Mourned

As we drove by the road kill,
Too slow to conceive their danger,
She spoke small blessings
At the carcasses slain
And flattened to shadows
Of self on immovable
Surfaces, concrete death

She passed this grief
Right on to me—
Existential osmosis?
That just may be—
I find myself counting
The casualties
And speaking for the dead,
Dead in the arrogance,
Ignorance, indolence of
The human sin of speed

I fear that one day I will
Pull on the fur of the skunk
For a cap, and attach
One undamaged crow
Wing above my left ear,
Slip on the deerskin
Over my shoulder,
The snapping turtle shell
On my chest for an armored plate,
A snakeskin around my throat,
And a fox pelt around my waist

116

Picture me then in the headlights,
A ghoul, a skin walker over
The road in a slow motion,
Drum beat, ancient as earth,
As the semis and sedans veer
For the ditch but cannot escape
The slow doom of my Mother's animal grief

***

The Fine Art of Motion

Missed the Art Show on Friday Night,
Went to a Birthday,
Caught in a card game at the kitchen table,
In too deep and could not quit
Suddenly, up to my nose in bad cards
We're planning a trip to Grandfather
Mountain, North Carolina, now!
The fine art of motion,
The expression of living,
Defeats the Art on the wall every time
It takes some time to pay the house
And slow the journey down—to see

***

Japanese Poem At Beaverwart Academy
Bone Town University, 2012

Stand up from the flush in the unisex bathroom,
Humanities Building, the breaking coffee waters at noon
Turn to the sink
And there are two rose petals,

Perfect as a Japanese poem,
Against the porcelain white,
The melancholy of 10,000
Murakami novels
Makes me chuckle down in my crusty heart
I am a sucker for the bones of fine art

***

So Mammal; So Exposed

Last Sunday I saw a car against the wall of the 3rd Street
    overpass—
Car bite wall and busted axle—
There were two patrol cars on the street below the mess,
None above—
There was no such thing as traffic control—
I drove past, slowly-
No one was cuffed in the cruiser's back seat—
The driver and passenger's doors hung wide...

What did I see, stuck up in my face,
 In front and back of both wrecked car seats?
Two big, wide, ham hunked uniformed butts—
I have a lot to investigate too—
But I hope I do not use that posture
In my investigations, hmm?
So mammal, we end up so exposed-

***

Holy Chore

Once I learned to fork the silage from the sweet manure hole
Up in the box, so we could haul it off to the cows

Now I do this exercise in my heart,
Forks full of shit from the sins of my past
Tossed in the black mouth of tomorrow
To feed my future and seek a fertile place

***

This Is The Present

That was not snow we saw this morning—
The rain was so happy it splashed the
World with the transubstantiation of matter
In a glittering gauze to protect the
Naked, barely greened up earth—
This is the present, a gift to April 15th

***

Pray That These Words May Rise

Four adult geese and a gaggle,
Casting off from the sand and rocks,
They head out on to the blue grey water,
Pointed at the dark tree line-
The tree line jagged like a good landscape
Artist would paint them—
Actually, those folks do the kind of sailing I would like—
Nice picture—are you sure those are geese?
I think they might be group of ancient Bretton
Monks on a journey,
On their way north to Canadian Avalon
In fact I am pretty much convinced of it—who lies?

The poet? Your eye?
Or is it the poverty of language

In an empirical, heretical world:
So that even words must rebel in
Order to speak out on behalf of the universe?
Like the geese or monks on the water,
I pray that these words may rise from
The void of this white Paper Lake and fly

***

What We Keep

Last time you were here
You astounded the little boy by eating the
Canadian cherries off the tree
Now he is as tall as you,
It is a cold spring, and the petals of the blossoms
Blow like scales of cream
Off the same tree in the North West wind that should
Have ended in March,
And you will head back to China

This is not ironic—
Age is more than seasons; time is less than death
Beware the gifts of the rich—

They sour;
Poverty is bitter, but only for a while—
Eternity is what we keep

Dagon, an old god, chats with the new neighbor.

Relocating God—Introduction

So what is God telling you?
I don't know: I see the things I am shown.
What is the theme?
What is the theme, you say?
What is the main idea?
Well, what is the theme of a melody? God's theme is a
    melody.
You hear it, hate it, love it, and tear it—now sing it.
God talks to us in music
Yes, it is true. All of those songs in the bible,
Those hymns and psalms, the parables, prophesies,
That handwriting on the wall, the cross "On a hill far
    away..."
Does this mean we shrug off 2000 years of faith?
    I don't know. I hear the Words and sing them.
I am asking you to explain your faith.
He who has ears (she too) let him (her too) hear.

***

Re-locating God—Godric

1

The boy picked up a damaged, half-dead butterfly off the hot
    parking lot:
Down, look down, he did

He let it go; it flapped one winged if that, a floundering flutter
    onto concrete:
Down, look down, he said

You can't help anything, he says to me, unless it helps you to:
People, even people—
Up, look up, he did

2

The fire smolders from bad wet wood
Godric sits with a 5-foot pole in hand,
Stirs up the fire in the pit of his dream
The mud and grass and trees are dark
If he looks up through the leaves
And the branches of the ash
He can see some stars

Too shadows slide across the grass behind him
He appears, like a horse at night, to doze,
And the shadows slip in quickly,
Godric stands and shouts out, SHEKINAH!!!
Slaps the pole against a shadow's head
And stabs the pole into the other shadow's face—
One shadow lays there, silent—
The other curls into a ball,

Holds the place a head would be and moans—
Godric leans above the shadows and speaks:
"Tell the princes of your world I bring the sign of Jonah."

Then he walks out from underneath the trees
Through the mud up to the road
And the summer Milky Way opens wide above

3

Oh, around midnight, in a dark dank ditch
Just after midnight on a dark, paved road
South of a vapor streetlight town,
Up in the north central part of the county,
Some wanna-be poet has his Godric dream

This is a dream: what happens to granite grey—
Shaded wolf dog or large coyote saunters
Across the scoria road,
Up from one shallow rabbit-less ditch
And down into the other
This is the dream of a clear summer night, no moons
Above the dark paved scoria edged up road that ran
North and south on the compass root
Below where the Big Dipper seemed ready to dump
Itself out on a hazy glowing spot ahead: the town

Something moved again in the ditch
A man, a shadow, a dog, a grey shadow man
With a five foot pole in his boney hands
He stepped out onto the black streak of road
And seemed to float more than walk
Tacking to the north, the pole a rudder to steer

The Milky Way was fresh and bright,

Flowing, streamed in a thick white gauze, like wind
Its south end reached for the Rocky Mountain chain
And the north tip touched Lake Winnipeg's southern point

4

Early light on gravel glistens, dew and sun and dust
Beneath the dreamer's feet
There are the glass tipped grassy bladed lawns-
One bee vibrates, invisible pressure
Inches from the dreamer's nose
The dream is real, and the bee still stings
A distant car rushes and shushes the highway,
But not too much, too near
A lone mighty bullfrog solos on his bass
Stain glass window wing glossed flies
Pretend they are dragons active on earth,
Gold in light, in shadow, then in sun
Conversational crows talk big, first thing,
Braggarts yet to fail

The NW breeze is lightly iced
Rubber tires and gravel pop
And hush, and pop again
Screened off from the dream
By faded green leafed, tight barked
Straight young bowing ash rows
One, lone, chrome blue dragon
Lights and rises, lights and rises,
From tip to tip of gleaming grass
All these things do seem to know
Exactly what and where they are
I sit in a daze and know
That if I face straight east into the light
That stirs the molecules of frozen air

My whole "Zoe" will peek out from my guts
And raise my faith from out beneath
The bill of my sneaky cap,
Out from behind these hoodlum shades
Faith wills me out to see just what
The dream wreck of God will do today!

5

It is still you, you same old gold, you dragon's mite
That lands like an angel on the edge of this book?
This part of the book is about Ojibwa nouns,
Verbs, and the fact that the nouns and verbs
Refuse to make beings into objects
You hook your four majestic little legs
On the top of the left hand leaves of the book
I vibrate with glee and then learn to sit still
Your body is long, an actual creamy white,
With gold and honey stripes,
Thin horizontal/vertical geometrically solid lines
Your stained glass wings of silver and gold
Are out, full length, a vibrating motor of God
Your head is as big as an Irishman's
With eyes the black of a deep down well: on me
We sit; your body relaxes; the wings droop down,
At rest—I breathe—you tense up—I sit
You relax and appear to look in me
We sit this way for minutes—I was tricked by light
Your wings are really translucent, not stained,
But gold, with white tint sketched in curving lines

We share no message but, maybe, "rest"—I read
Then at the bottom of the page,
I hesitate; I look; you look at me
I turn the page; you fly,

125

And in the ruins of our peace,
A huge black gleaming monster with two-inch wings
Like rotary blades,
With the sound from the shuffle of a brand new deck,
Floats like an inter-dimensional mission right into my face
Reflex lifts my hand—I shift—It leaves
Noun and verb, no subject is an object
Dragons, do we absorb the light,
Or is it light that finally swallows us?

6

Godric, God's wreck, Fredric Buckner saith,
God's Rick go the distance and wake up to your life
A paved lane leads north between the rows of poplar
From the lake and into fields, groves and towns
A last great blue dragon hangs in humid late afternoon
Above a puddle of muddy water
It rained hammer, tongs, and lightning frogs, all
Hard-edged nouns and verbs pounded down and down
For three stations of the cross—early, late last night
Who knows how long or what the distance even means?
Eternity is…what is this? My eyes can't see the word.

7

No, the word's not "clouds", but "waves";
Whites and yellows (ivory)—
Translucent (meaning I can't see)
Paved road embedded with 10 million bits of gravel,
Mowed on the margins—a line of thirty foot poplars runs—
The eastern breeze, not humid today,
The long, lingering, loosely laid out Egyptian cotton,
Thin sheets of light lay down across the grass,
The trees, the road.

Here in the shade, I can see the sun,
But the sun seems reddish and not too warm-
The huge golden brown dragon flies
Mimic the flight patterns of insects they eat in hordes—
Fine with me, amazing balance,
As long as I am not the one in the dragon's jaws.
I wait and doze and know we all will wake.

8

I hear one goose, maybe two
Through the trees,
Across the road
In the pot hole near the lake
One awkward "Conk!" and then a "Honk" or two.
Beautiful glory of Sunday deep on October's edge
Before we make my head all busy
And ruin the silent angel songs.
Angelic being, tell me what I need to know:
"Conk! Honk!" and I'm left awake to ponder all this webbed
     in blue,
Webbed and wandering, cool in denim faded and soft Mary
     Blue.

***

The Vonnegut Bird

I know I have told you about this bird before
Named it The Vonnegut Bird this winter
I never see it, but I thought its Po to weet
Which I heard, in the cold of me ears
As so it goes, so it goes,
And I felt like Billy Pilgrim
This winter it's down to two syllables

Pt twwet pt twweet—It goes it goes
But then it seemed a question—
What goes? What Goes?
This morning it was clear a sentence
In one of Vonnegut's books
Here in this small town
On the edge of the end of the world
The bird clearly said, let's Go, let's go
And something inside me went
When will we high plains creoles out
Here take the chance to know who we are
Identity is a single word

***

Ear Comedy Folk Songs

What songs I do know come by ear
It's just the way I learned
I learn by touch, the oil of pores
Pours from my tongue and finger tips
And out the heart hound pounded
Nerves and veins through drummed and
Drowned in blood in touch and finger tips;
And from the (Hebrew) "Fundament"
The base of spirit, ruddy "RUAHHHH"
Rears and tumbles from my throat
And out my lips—
The unknown comes to know
From those eternal notes, found words,
To float, to strum and drum, to sing
Beyond the speed of brain
Through human heads and hearts
Into the lord's all-known ear,
Ear comedy, and balladry, providential blues,

Heal, improvise, remember, see,
Members, human family,
Melody to voice on air, 6 strings,
Divined, but when It's done
It joins the choirs of God's own
Time and space torn angel psalms—
Gospel, comedy, country blues,
Closer to the Coming Kingdom's tunes

***

1

Now in the deep dead February steel,
When Epiphany green will freeze back brown
And before you wear the mixed ashes of
Oak, fir, holly, ivy and mistletoe,
Here comes Saint Brighid's dream

On the corner of North Broadway and University Avenue
    West,
The tax office is hot for hell;
Taxes time's taxes, all money axes taxed,
Unless you have an accountant who knows the big numbers
That makes debits appear in a credible way.
Who do I see as I piddle by in exhaust streams
On a blue skied, ice blue afternoon
(With a nice brisk snap the skin to bleed in a NW wind
That makes Old Glory above the building stand stiff
As a Marine Private's parts, San Diego Saturday night)?
Well, I see a 5-foot animate, humanoid,
Moss green dancing Statue of Liberty in a black mask—
(Her) little triangle pointed crown droops down in front of
    her face.
They're beside her, a bowl full of pudding,

Red cheeked, stocking caped,
Red and black check flannel shirted white bearded
Blue eyed gnome dances too
He's about as tall as middle school kid.
They are talk and bounce, bounce up and down to keep
    warm.
What do you suppose I will do?
I just pull into the parking lot,
Zip up my lousy military tent of a parka,
Jog over to them to ask for an interview.
Santa, his red cheeks bouncing, with a brown tobacco juice
    stain in his beard,
He says, "Interview?
For the paper? Where's the camera? Just what for?"

Then Liberty with her flopping crown,
Whips out a digital ink-pen tape recorder,
Glares up at me, and smiles at Santa Claus:
"Ready, steady to go. It is all recorded."
Flannel Santa pulls out a notebook and big lead pencil,
One of those flattened, wide-lead carpenter's deals,
A big red one—he licks it and says,
"What do you want to tell us?"
I shiver: paranoia trumps the cold—
I look around for an unmarked van,
A camera hidden in Liberty's flopping crown.
She looks sinister, deadly behind the black mask.
"I just wanted to know, to see,
What the two of you were doing out here in this weather,
On this kind of day. I wanted answers from you."
I am now bouncing in place with them in a trio,
But they face off against me, strong, aggressive formation.
"Well, we will interview you instead; that's the deal!"
He snarls into his brown stained beard.
He pulls out a sheaf of papers and shoves them at me.

"Are those your words?" he says.
"What," I stutter, cold and alone, all of a sudden,
Barely able to hold three nicely typed sheets
Of paper in my freezing red chapped hands.
These gloves are useless.
"Don't bother to fling them into the wind,"
Liberty says from behind her eerie black nylon mask,
"Because we made many copies."
I peruse the short, clearly typed bytes of prose,
Nicely bracketed by quotation marks.
"Yes, they are my words, but out of context, clearly"
I say as the warm air clouds out of my mouth
And I suck in a prison-cold sack full of ice and exhaust.
Liberty stares into my eyes: "completely?"
"No. Not completely, all out of context."
"But you said these words in these sentences in this order?"
"Yes." She sneers at me, says, "Be quiet",
Then turns to Red cheeked Santa and says,
"What else do we need?"
"A signature," he says as he unwraps a cheap
Imitation Congressional cigar with the tips of his short red
    fingers.
"What?" I blurt as I step back from them and find myself
    looking
Around in the bright, frozen toxic light.
I am trying to locate a solid spot in real time.
Liberty pulls a large yellow sheet of paper
Embossed with a the drawing of a gnawing beaver
And words in red and green, ink—
She points with her pen at a blank, black line:
"The confession, the signed confession—
The one you sign," and shoves it into my chest
As I stumble back in fear and see Santa moving behind to
    block me.

Then the bright, frozen, carbon monoxide street corner
    world goes black.

2

The Golden haired goddess
Makes three great fires:
The hammer and fire of the sword maker,
The chant and beat of the word warden's call,
And the healing drug of the summer spell—

Dress in white and blood red too—
Hear Brighid's song— smithies pull steel out of the fire,
The sacred words of poem and dance
Layered steel and rising light—
Hard forged in slavery's night
Long day of light eternal come to stay
All of these prophecies hang in the black
Empty death and the star shot cold

And earth, this scarred and grimy cast
Iron pot that yearns to be silver and live,
Yes earth waits for that long light day—
Sharpen your pencils—only hard forged words will do

Here is what Nietzsche says about professional philosophers.
They do a "critique of words by means of other words."
To which I say, "What else would we use? Machine guns?"
What was old Fred thinking?
Like this: "Words, just words and more words
—Let me see you put your words into act."
I reply, "And what were your actions,
That your words should be worth more than others?"
He would say, "I started World War Two and killed God—
Not bad for a mediocre Lutheran, ech?"

"Was that before or after the sex bug got you down?" I say.

It's like Henry David Thoreau: "If Walden was so great, why
    were you always sneaking on over to Concord for Sunday
    Dinner and such?"
To which he says, "It was the quality of my active time,
    planting, building my home, walking and walking off
    those pots of home-grown beans."

Hammer the sword blade in the fire—
Brew the magic healing broth from
Moss, bark and leaves of summer light—
The planets are moving in step dance reels—
The sun and moon protect us from Mars—
God ignite St. Brighid's three fired power soon
"And it says to me, dear listener to my thoughts,
That if I want to find the Kingdoms of light,

I will be hammered on Her anvil,
Made pliant as heated steel in her horribly hot old fire.
Then I will dowsed in a bucket,
A liquid solution of healing green things, purple mosses,
Roots of strange dog wood bushes, and healed—
Then, She might allow me to know enough about when
To speak and what to say so that I might write some poem of
    praise."

***

Jobs are worth nothing if they eat the center—
I have never had a real "job" for long
I was a priest for a long, strange storied while—but that was
    just a call—
Jobs are a service to the Universe, at their very best—
Any job that's helpful to the world,

133

Any Christian or Zen knows that—
At their worst, the jobs make slaves,
Meaningless and mean, destructive of the worker,
With work that kills the meat of soul—
Materialism comes to sin—
Marx and Smith both fail—
Karl and Adam give us dirt, pollution,
Sin, paralysis: of the holy flow of life

The Marx boys and Smith Brothers provide
A service, sooth the throat and make us laugh—
Their healing work still sets the children free
Hearts pound with laughter,
Throats are cleansed to sing the Word—

But Karl and Adam, boys did you go wrong,
And you can't blame this on Eve!

The Flesh was made Word, and our flesh,
By grace of God's own song, can sing the "the Word made
     fresh"*,
Again, and then again

— Larry Woiwode

***

I Heard Someone Calling, Saul, and Wept

The play was played and the lost act done—the director?
Unconscious in a bath tub full of Ever Clear and Florida
     oranges
     The banquet went on long past the winter dawn
Next to the table, filled with fresh organic fruit and wine,
A young man said to his young man friend,

This is my point about macaroni and cheese, you see
Someone at my elbow spoke:
"The wind towers
remind me of the wings of geese in flight"
but when I turned to thank him
he was walking out the door
the women in my face just sighed and said,
my oil pumps remind me of ancient things
I shrugged and murmured, no the pumps
are pumping ancient things, but the pumps are new
so she drank off her glass of wine and smirked,
and those B 52's in flight at dawn?
They are vultures, pure above the plains,
and I hedged, I growled,
vultures clean organic garbage up
those planes leave nothing there to clean
she gave up and turned away
just as I saw a sunlight polished glimmer
on the knob and wood of a light pine door
I opened the door to walk outside
and stepped into a closet, clothes and glue
I panicked, backed up, hit the door,
found the knob, stepped out again
and walked like Morrison down the hall
out the front door and into the clouds,
but the sun was bright as the armor of Gawain
blinded, I tripped and fell
I heard someone calling, Saul, and wept

Yeah, poetic justice has its drawbacks—we do not get to see
    it—is that what makes it poetic or what makes it justice?

Sitting with coffee
the sun gets a day to work
before the next snow

light across the valley
makes me think of sitar
strings—Ravi is handy,
and as I pull out the disk
I see he was right beside
George, and George is
sitting neck deep in blue water
suddenly it's 1965
and I walk out at the end of
"Help" at the Play House Theater
there in the Spot,
and the world is wide open,
one long Beatles chase scene
It is not old age I fear
not even death
It is the same fear of
1965, before the war
killed 4 friends
It is the fear that we
do not matter
I close my eyes
listen to the raga
roll across my head
open my eyes
and another river valley
is drunk with orange
winter sunlight
My heart runs, Ravi,
My heart runs, George
right along the planes, plains
of winter sun, here, comes...
hear comes, and that is all we need

One thing we never understand—"I" am not "YOU"—
He is not She—You are not me,

They do not exist and we are very temporary in almost every
    case-
-That is called the grammar of grace—
I do not fit your shoes, polished or scuffed,
And you do not wear my perfect bra—

***

Pamela's parents were North Dakota lean,
silk and muscle wrapped around bones of cottonwood
with nervous systems made of barbed wire and rose thorns
When they went to Chicago to dance with Lawrence Welk,
he gave them a magnum of good champagne
But the Al Capone asked Pamela's mother to dance,
and she politely told him to forget it pal,
so one of his thugs made threats— You know
who he is? You better let him dance with yer wife pal
And Pamela's father told him to walk out behind the barn
There was no murder and mayhem
They got on the bus for North Dakota
Lawrence went on to LA and Public TV
Al went to St Valentine's day and the IRS
Goes to show what barbed wire, cottonwood,
silk and rose thorns can do

Snow on snow, white on brown and grey snow,
Two chimneys blowing smoke,
One dog barks, two big old crows tease,
The dog barks back,
And along freight whistles down by
The riverbanks below us

One woman says, "Well she goes to UND
And is in a sorority with a frat partner,
And they always have stuff going on,

And I say, well we have oil here in Bone Town"

Somewhere the day will end with the sun out,
Some kind of same old pastel patient colors,
Maybe some music or a book somewhere
And God will not blink but bless some deed
Done somewhere here in the limestone basin
Where any thing but keeping on is far
From clear, clean, open, easy, free or real

Do not go into the Cock with a loaded gun!!!!
The cock he struts, acts like he's nuts or has
Too many nuts to spare
Then he gets drunk and pulls a gun
For barroom truth or dare
The coppers come and take him down
Cold cell, wet underwear
The little cocks like great big guns
And now you little cocks, beware!!!!
We'll find a place where you all fit
And pack you all

It makes those molecules dance
New life is the end we find begins

I wrote the supernatural love story set in ND
It is called Ballads from The Spot
you are in it—and you mandolin
and your odd woman, and your cool aid
popcorn Twilight Zone tests
but I think it had another name
I think we all had another name
I think now is the time to make
the book into a movie of
oily proportions and golden light

from a man's veins and bloody,
bleeding out into the earth of
the west while the pumps on the
pads release the natural gas
and the black blood from the
geological spirits of ten billion
plants and animals waiting
for resurrections, remembrance
and less wretched burial conditions
In the mean time we will be on
the back porch and the mandolins
and guitars with be chiming like
church bells made of wood and wire
out across the valley and prairie
and into the bowels of creation
while we drink the red wine in the
wind and sunshine of last summers

New life is the end we find begins

I wanna sit in the sun in Daubigny's garden,
Sit and play my guitar
And have a grandma and child walk by
And no even know who they are
And share my song with their bread and cheese
And my bottle of read wine
And here that grandma sings in French,
In between my lines

Lemons, ice, water, white wine,
A blue bowl and Vincent staring at the cypress trees—
Heaven is made of colors like these

***

The Luck of The High Plains Creole

NOT sure this is what I meant—cool White dude with stick
    and stones
Ah, the Purple of Lent in February—not Luck my friends,
Not luck at all but the wisdom of a king on a cross—
February Birthday is the day of the pansy light

Well, me and a bunch of other knot head heads with stick
    and stones
Still live in this state,
My dear girl, My Goddess testifies—ND ain't really safe!

A secret Artist paints out of the pansy's soul
Here is the inside of my guts—kinda purty, no?
This sacred stuff that makes me flux and free
Darwin and the Old brown "Fundamental—Soul";
Hebrew prophet saw the same things,
And neither of them had fiber optic eyes!!!!

My Wife Looks Like this every day at Sunrise—
Roots, messed and glowing in the light of sleep and sun
Now I know the clear bright Why!!
Nothing to do, bow down to glory, Wisdom—
She is the magic, not the doubt!

Sickness knows no political party
Let us build a black oiled calf onto ourselves a
ND calls us the North of Dakota,
Land, lost causes, greasy oil dreams—a
Black gold temple and a black gold parson's home
For the High Priest of Black gold
And worship unto them

Some of it makes it simple—God knows?

Or as Grandma said, there but for the grace of God go I
—Did not get it—now it gets me

And something deep inside me went
When will we high plains creoles out here take the chance
To fight to know our parent's dreams, and know just who we
    are?
Identity is one word—

This white out day of
Blow and bust and worship winds that pound the walls
And the word ain't luck—the Word ain't faith—It's grace

The Luck of The High Plains Creole (Again)

Ah, the things we do so we can keep our laptops plugged in
    —know why our leader will not stop this?
Because will not force them to stop this
A conference of Cardinals in the cloister of snow, ice and
    empty lines and trees
they pray, they vote, the watch smoke rise
and in the Ice of Christ they all are free
Read some history before you attack
the enemy and the enemy ends up being your self
Life lives on life—how pure do I feel now?
I am a piece of meat with a brain and a soul
and two hands to touch my guitar
My tribal lands have felt the shovel of hell
the gas of revolution
and the puking pewl of the popes
Great Mystery, Great Mystery;
we repeat ancient history until we see your hand now—
Look at the next person you see—
It still means I am kind of dumb,
but I am convinced that problems mean

141

I have been hard at work asking questions
A God could resolve,
and then I say, where is god,

And the whole thing tumbles down surprise!
Mirror! This is the super train idea, and notice that Montana,
Like your old home, does not exist for super trains—
Between the west coast and Minnihappyloss is no one's land,
And from Canada down to the central plains, same ting,
Mon—we de lost colonies!!! Until de want de
Coal, oil, gas, wheat, corn, canola, beef, chickins,
An mebe de wind, eh,
—Be cool, power rules, and we the underclass of fools

The Grammar of Surprise and Grace

Hadley, turning to Hemingway, said that She had a headache
—
Hemingway had Picasso's hat, and had to give it back—
Auden said, don't care how much you had,
It's what you have that matters and that too will be taken
        away—
This is the grammar of surprise and grace

NOT sure this is what I meant—cool White dude with stick
        and stones
Ah, the Purple of Lent in February—not Luck my friends,
Not luck at all but the wisdom of a king on a cross—
February Birthday is the day of the pansy light

Well, me and a bunch of other knot head heads with stick
        and stones
Still live in this state,
My dear, My Goddess testifies—ND ain't really safe!

142

A secret Artist paints out of the pansy's soul
Here is the inside of my guts—kind of purty, not?
Here in this small town
on the edge of the end of the world
the bird clearly said, "Let's Go. Let's Go,"
and something deep inside me went

The wrench in the gut
The slam in the door
As it cracks on the wall
When the sense
Of a Turkish patrol
Car pulled in front
Of your face when
The bribe is paid
By a Bob Dylan fan
With a dead guitar
And an urge to be
The one who takes?
The goddess down
To the end of the
Song where blood
Stains trail
To the side walk lines
And someone says
When you get your
Age you should know
Enough not to slam
The door when you leave

And you say,
Jesus is Lord of doors,
All tombs and Dawn
Redeemed isn't faith—It's grace
***

143

Political Wings

Back to the sunny window,
I see large bird shadows
Wing and swoop on the screen
And walls—shadow and light
Crows (it is winter),
Pigeons (it is Lent),
And then there is the
Shout of 10 million voices
In my baffled and baffling head:
The Kingdom is right now!
Turn around, look out the window!
See it coming on the clouds

***

Night Train

Keep ridin' that night train,
we all ridin' that night train,
in the key of I AM again,
gonna all be free but I don't know when—
-And the night train keeps on movin',
Three times since I been on,
Father, son and Holy Ghost will remember us when we're
       gone,
Riding that night train to Bone Town,
Ridin' that night train to magic,
Ridin' that night train to some place,
A quiet place with a mandolin
Strumming in the trees, to a place that looks
Enough like home to be our home again
***

Tennis and Sin

1

I seem to remember an avenue of oaks,
Sunlight and shadow on grass
As late afternoon sloped slightly
Beamed light
But, says Luther, "What does this mean?"
That sound of the tennis ball
Against the racquet,
Then court, then opponent's racket
This thing, win, lose,
The sweat and sweat breeze
September, defeat,
The half-dragged weapon,
The yellow balls against the fence
The sagging shoulder
Hanging heads

One black mountain bike
Leans against one oak
A bell rings from the campus across the street
And further up the hill
Yellow light is strained through
The leaves that still hold their green
Someone shouts the word "Out!"
And you can see clearly:
The ball was in—
Match point—what now?
The winner walks off along the line
And into the shade of the oaks,
Pulls off his cap, puts it back on,
Looks at a tree

Surely he knows he can lose the same way,
The next match or the one after that
This is what I mean
The loser drinks deep from his water jug
Only the judge is fooled by her call
The winner, the loser and everyone
Else can plainly see
The connection between
The tennis ball and the sin

2

At this late time of day
The metal mesh of the
Fence throws shadows
Out across the courts,
Along with tree trunks
And oak leaves
We have the yellow ball
Out in the light, shadow
Darkness, black and
Yellow off the court,
Hard for the heart of the swing
Hard to hold with the eyes
The human lens
Breaks down—the easy
Pride of young eyes
Caught in the shadows and light
The line at the taut high end
Of the net is strung to catch
The young athletes' eyes
The ball, a bird, a soul
Sin is a matter of too much
Trust in finite, fragile perception
It's not so simple, this:

"Just keep your eye on the ball"

3

As the air cools in long shadows
The blue team falls behind
4 to 0: our team's ahead again
So what is this sorrow, now?
Blue can to nothing right
We can be sloppy and win
The air is almost too cool,
The time of day you decide
To go back inside and
Put on a warmer coat
It is too cold out for snakes,
So what is this feeling that
Makes me keep an eye on the grass?
The score is back to 40 all
With a deuce and hard rally
The Blue team actually wins

"Either way," somebody says,
In the oracular tones of a preacher,
"Someone will lose,
So somebody has to win"
That clarion calls from the
Tower of the college across the street
"Calling the young and old to rest"
Some day the wins and the losses
All align, side by side, in stone
Should our team know that now?

***

You Are Not Your Own Guitar

Boys with guitars get girls he heard
And so began to strum,
Hammer, shout it out and finally
Learned to sing that heart beat
Feeling, harmony and strings caressed
Sure enough, along came girls
They fell in sound holes,
Wrapped like vines around the neck,
Caught the boogey woogie fever
From the curves of that guitar
And sacrificed, first tongues, then bodies,
Even hearts
Sliced like butter
On the strings
To the beat of that flat top guitar
They pounded passions
Beat drummed sounds,
But just for the guitar
Never for the boy who played
The boy? He loves to sit
Entranced, his fingers
Slipping, lover soft
The frets along the neck

The only woman he ever loved
Turned her back on many songs,
Burned his body deep with love
Whenever she desired
Kept him, keeps him,
Fire and oil, fire and ice,
And when he ponders this old song
She says, "It's simple
You are not your own guitar"

***

When you find a loose cart at the shopping mall
Rolling in a half circle in the wind
It's like the digital loops in your heads—
The man's loop plays a mix of mother and father;
Woman's loop plays a mix of father and mother—
The Child grows loops from tangled vines, mother and
Father in the turn of the wheels of the cart,
And when the child finds the body of woman and man,
The life of the universe continues to roll across
The parking lot between the black holes and planets
To the beat of a Bobby Dylan home sick blues—

I simply say that from the touch of the apple
To the teeth to the Whore of Babylon,
From Rush to Limbo and Osama,
The Creator of the multiverse
Will never give us up, and those of us,
Take me for one, implicated in the worst of sins,
Is as much a driving force in the story
As the greatest saints—
Salvation and Damnation, described from any human
Point of view, are both beyond my ken,
Sinner and repeat offender that I am,
"Leaning, leaning, leaning on the everlasting arms",
Eve all the way to the Omega,
At the foretold stories' end—
I tire of the issue being
"Who gets damned today" instead
Of that grand "Magnificat", the tale we call the Bible—
I am waiting, truly, for the Man—there is nothing else—
In mean times I sin, a fool in rags of grace,
In the hope the Wisdom I call God pertains to me and mine

149

Mother: something I can hear and understand,
Even though now as I am, I understand it all
Son: how about this? Why can't Koehler
Make a sink drain that holds the water
When you want it held, and lets
The water go when you are done?
Mother: always the same since the world was broken
And water taught to run through pipes
Son: or why Mother, now that I am older,
Does it bother me to call for a Doctor's appointment
And have the childish sounding voice demand to know:
"Date of birth", and why do I feel weaker?
Mother: It wouldn't help to tell you
"None of these things matter";
I remember my own death so well,
How much it mattered then, to me.

***

Between Finite and Infinite, Conclusion

What color would blood have to be?
To make those in power cry at the pain they inflict
On the helpless in freedom's name?

What sound will the hard heart sing?
To create regret
In the arrogance of the rulers?

How many songs
Will we have to sing
Before we raise the dead?

There will be songs.

The saints will rise up
When we fools lift up our heads.

Remember salvation
In the valley of bones,
And then the bones will rise.

***

Syllogistics

1.   The pheasant roosters in the shelterbelts of the
      campground crow at each other all evening until it is
      cold enough for campfires.
2.   The sign on the bath house wall says: Ft Stevenson
      State Park Frontier Days—Frontier Army of the
      Dakotas—Arikara Scouts—'Black Power' Rifle Firing
      Demonstration
3.   In 1968, Pastor Haakinson up dated bible study with
      current events—young and old gathered—as we
      shouted relevant current events out from our chairs,
      he scribbled them on the board—Adolf Schwarzen,
      who later ran this preacher out of town in a German
      explosion of piety, raised his hand and asked, "What
      does 'Black Powder' have to do with all of this? They
      don't even use it in veaponz any moor"
4.   The connections words make or unmake shape the
      life of the soul. Adolf is dead and has an answer for
      his entire question. The congregation is dying, and
      the Stone Church could soon be an empty Ein Feisty
      Burg on the hill by the County Jail.

From Hopes of Tom M.

Our behavior at Christmas was always the same:
Go get the tree, drag it back home in the pickup
Or in the trunk of the car,
Hang it with memories so that your eyes
Glitter with twinkling tinsel and
Lights of past-loved grief, nostalgia or both; so helpless—
Then water it as if to make the poor green grow.

Ever since Herod massacred baby boys for Christmas
In an effort to murder that star-grazed King,
There is something out of kilter about the
Tree, no matter how carefully placed in the stand.

Two planets were
Hung up on the hooks of a moon
At the solstice of my 12th year.
I had almost died for my birthday.
I did not know the dying and rising gods.
Mithras/Maat slept in the cottonwoods
Down south of the house by the Cannonball.
The cattle and sheep would not behave.

I grew up in a town that believed in God,
But I wasn't sure God believed in me:
Trite but not bad for a near-dead
12-year-old failed football guard with a transistor radio
Pressed to his ear early on Christmas Day,
Under the blankets with KOMA
At three AM in the morning,
Wondering at life and his newly
Repaired "coarctation of the aortic artery".

...Because it is the premise of many acknowledged scholars that Christianity created capitalism. I subscribe to that thesis. —Ralph Kingsbury, Grand Forks based economist (GF Herald, 12/07)

1.	A PHD +tenure+emeritus status might=apollonian-disinterested angling intellect, further abuse of a "Terminal Degree".

2.	Now the economist "steppes" out of the not so red but frozen river of academic ice flows, out of the valley of the red north with his neo- conservative, Calvino-Baptist civil-sized crypto-historical religious rah-rhetoric and it floats him, Wise man on his way to a religious right up against the Wall Mart, above the uncritical post-Christmas masses:

3.	Christianity invented Capitalism, because it happened to be around, i.e., Jews lent money to Kings and Popes who took care of the Pesky Jews with pogram and penned them in ghettos, banks, interest, guilders for guilds, industrial revulsion, bonds, non- payment, university, 3rd degree—economics invented Adam Smith (who said that plenty meant that if you had three linen shirts you would surely give one to your needy friend next door); why not Marx as well, and Hitler too (a Catholic/Lutheran Grail freak), some one to blame for the deaths of 6 million Jews?

4.	And on we go with the bollixed, post-modern logical branding, naming, digging, computerized, digital Blog-slog gut-stewed slaughter of fact and fiction both.

5.	Adam Smith, stand aside: It's the fault of Shakespeare and the 'Merchant of Venice', "...a pound of flesh, tis not so much!"

6.   So Jesus, Mary and Martha sat, right after the Sermon on the Mount, and invented capitalism den and der, cigars and brandy at their sides.

7.   Or old St Paul, who linked the body and blood of Christ with the offering taken for the poor—was he a commie?

8.   Jesus the failed capitalist gave it all away, and Zaint Paul, seeing the blinding light, "...the good that I would do I don't..." "...by faith through grace...all will have 401k's..."?

9.   Right, not St Paul neither.

10.   I know, it was after that Constantine, before the French Revolution, I know them bishops and popes and mini-bishes out to grecify the doctrines, out to plotinize them creeds, out to solidify the solid state and holify them virgins—didn't they introduce the interest rates, the golden standard, the credit line, the market in unlimited futures?

11.   Not! Says Adam and Adam Smith rolling over in their graves, not at all, and what you call capital-ism ain't (read Smith his self)

12.   Who was it then, dealed the dollar, barreled the oil, blew off the bombs of fair market value, the stamp of meaning on human toil, the fact of this meaningless dollar-me dime-me nickel-me lead coated penny to death: it's billions and billions dese days my girl!

I grew up at Christmas in a town where we all had much of nothing, while Bob Dylan was still "blowing in the wind" somewhere over in the red hills of Hibbing: farmer, bank teller, preacher, teacher, cowgirl, clerk, hired girl, rancher nun or priest— and we still had more than we knew what do with our time—Joe and Anne Hersh at the Pheasant Café, Vince in his Cadillac, pink in front of the Log Cabin Bar, Red Watson, red with fire of work, war and love in the cab of his red tilt cab Ford hauling coal to farmers through the snow where the railroad wouldn't go, or Bob Carvell at the Rexall Drug—At St Vincent Church on the Eastern hill, Or Trinity Lutheran out on the west and all them little houses of holy stretched out on the soles of 2000 souls, on Christmas Eve we had too much and more, in spite of Commies Capitalist Cold War bull!!! Smoke that you Economics reducer of love and soul—

Jesus, Et Al EL,
Weren't much for money and things?
The Christ in us all
Is a bandito stealing souls from the Devil
Cross making fellers,
Edge of languages tale telling fellers,
Shift of the hand in the wind
Hang with the bad kids
Bring down the Counting house,
Who would just as soon drive the Devil,
The explainers of banking,
The revel-lution sellers—out the doors of the earthen temple

Jesus, he'll settle, the son of a man, Man,
For nothing less than Eden back at the
Homestead, summer camp small town ranch.

That Christmas back in the Spot
Kennedy and God were not forgot.
I heard the howling out on the snow
Blessed prairie:
"That ain't no ghost of Sitting Bull,
Them ain't no coyotes,"
Magdalena, my Great Grandma Said,
"I hear the holy hounds of heaven calling,"
And then she smiled and closed her eyes.

Theories on the star of Bethlehem
(Astrophysicist thinks 'Sign' was unusual alignment of planets)
=The advantage (Grant) Mathews has over the astronomers is that he had access to NASA's databases. (Grand Forks Herald 12/07)

There was no theory until Aristotle quoth: "let there be a scientist and a method"
The Sign was so mysterious; only three astrologers; Pershun, Hindoo and Boodhist;
Say they saw it—and frightened shepherds, and some sheep, maybe, and one wild Druid named Smokey Water far off in Ireland/Friesland/Prussia/Scotland Dakotah.

An unusual alignment? Tell that to Mary and Joseph, all misaligned himself or herself, "It was an angel she says," and he says, "…any one is an angel if he looks younger than me!"

Advantage: observable data makes a theory shot backwards, 2000 years or so.

Matthew, without the NASA data base, will tell you what Luke says, while John Saw it All Before: "In The Beginning was the WORD, and Mark saw no star at all: "They were afraid"; Astro-Mathews has it figured out—the economic NASA OH so holy story—the doctrine of bedrock bottom—

It ain't the data, Mathews, with one "t" missing from your game.
It ain't the data, it's the tale, and the tally is in the tale my star charts tell me true.

In the town where I learned Christmas, the star shown every
    year,
And Jesus lurked in the shelterbelts and snowy fields
Like the great glowing Cock that no hunter would ever
    shotgun.
He was still crowing in April when we got the news of Easter,
As eternal as monsignor Mandre's black cigar,
As tall as the Holy Blue Water Tower by Saint Vincent
    Church,
As clear as a the view from the top floor County Courthouse
    Windows
Where de victims of LAW looked down at the windy white
    Christmas streets.
Not all the girls in that spot were as lovely as Sheila,
Or immortals like Suzanne.
Some were as skinny as dangling ropes,
Some marked with pox, noses of India rubber,
Some big enough to straw boss the class
And take on the job of an entire baling crew,
So big they could break our entire football team.
There was power and glory in those mistaken farm girls.
Us funny boys, afraid of those girls,
Stuck our noses deep in Bee Jones' jelly donuts
And hid from the majestic, giant, great women they were.

I look down at my hands,
The strange broken lands here where
My public and private word songs form

Then I look out at this morning;
That tap of a hammer, near, down the hill
Below our house; a knock on a spruce wood top;
A sound like Neruda's voice from the southland of the soul,
From the other side of life:
"Wake up on the flesh strung chords of your guitar"

I open the black case, a sacramental tool kit black,
Touch the strings, and the key of G opens
Down into the cave that leads to life.

Or end like this:

In October
The numbers that trapped me
Melted into the leaves
From cottonwood branches,
Mud, early snow,
Then melted, water,
And these gold soaked
Afternoons
With the sharp, cold,
Crushed, rose petal rose,
Long slanting sunset,
Homer propped with a beer at the bar—
The smell of mold and sleep—the silence
Pulled into the night and an early frost
Left to shine silver—mornings are
Blue, left over lilac blossom
From the bushes across the
Road last June

Somehow their blooming injects their blue
Across this slowly shadowed purple valley—
A side spearing piercing lance of light,
And silence—one long curved note
On the highest of high E strings

Sooner or later, we all kiss the bearded lady

Cold Drinks at Eben-Nezer's,
   -or-
   Friends, Neighbors & Lovers at The Spot.

Lost Colony: By Line

"South Dakota Ghost town
Sold to church: future uncertain"
She reads aloud, looks up at me
And says,
"Is there a poem in there"?
And so there is, lost colony, colonolized again
But I am lucky,
Caught up as I am in wild space,
My lover's lips, her face, her bones and eyes
Seduced, I forget the historical boomtown blues

***

The Distinctive Moment of Artistic Recognition…

…A poem itself—

There on the old library table in the
Staff room of the Humanities Division
The cardboard container holds
Two half-eaten sweet rolls,
Two untouched; by teeth, at least,
And one dead fly that makes a smile;
Inked on the box, the following invitation:
"Help yourself, from The Post Modern Class"

    ***

The Price of the Poem
(For Debra Marquart)

Nothing can atone for the insult of a gift given
But the forgiveness of the one who receives
—Chinese Proverb translated in
S. W. North Dakotan (that sheepherder west of Mott)

I did not ask for the gift of your poem.
I did not need the parable your story made.
There was no cry for brandy satori.
I stayed—you left.
I am not always really here.
You were never really gone.
So here is the payback of the gift
From the stage of a bar in Dickinson
In 1971—("Keep your eyes on the road,
And your hands upon the wheel"—Jimmy Morrison),
To the fertile manure of Dog Town,
Just north the black hole they call Des Moines.

I lived among'em—as do you,
Iowa State, where the Student Union
Passes for Dracula's castle,

And the pigs root in the hot smell
Of pink porkish joy.

Here are my prayers and prairies
Dumped in your lap.

I pick up my Martin,
Walk out in front of kids 1/3 my age
And hear Bono say,
"OK Edge, play the blues!!!"
And I play them,
The Mott Dog, Mott Squad,
Ageless cottonwood blues.

***

When the blackbirds sweep in with the cold spring rain,
And the green grass sprouts up through the cracked brown
    clay,
The grey man's up and dancing with the Queen of May.
And do you know the Queen of May?

Fiddle me an ancient tune underneath the Easter moon.
Flute me out a nighthawk song.
Play the nighthawk all night long.
String it on the wood guitar:
Steel string, eternal hearts.
Will you be my May queen tune underneath the Easter
    moon?

Church, I don't know—
Tell my congregation
That a typical late winter Lent is stupid
Unless we dig up Jesus' bones,
And my hope was that Jesus

Will dig up our bones someday,
Along with all the other parts,
Every being on the planet,
In the universes for that matter—
The jury is still out—
I may have over-cooked the Easter Ham a bit—
Say, who was the old priest that smoked the big cigars?
I deeply admired him, and I don't think it was Mandrake was
    it?
He walked Main Street with that black cigar
And blessed us all with a prophet's hot coal
On the stuttering high pains tongue: holy smoke,
And the fact that things we couldn't see
Were going on all around us—even the Lutheran kids.

This town is the right size now.
Sunrise catches the upper window
Of the field stone Lutheran church on the
West side of the valley,
And by trick of creation's design
Morse code flashes
To the burnt tan brick St. Vincent Catholic Church
About one mile away
On the eastern ridge.
"Hello; hello; share this
Silence with me.
No one need see our sweet joint efforts
As we bless this town."

***

Here as proof is the tree
In pure rock... Pablo Neruda (35)

We played cowboys and Indians in

"Petrified Wood Park" in Lemmon SD,
Or "Combat" in the cottonwoods by the
Cannonball south of our house,
Where kids in kid's books play,
Not on the grassy plains all around us.

In the Petrified Wood temple
We were the priests,
Ritual makers of elegant faith,
We'd climb the plinths and dance
On the stone step trails,
Almost innocent little
Human guardians, cousins
By blood and
Protectors of stone bones,
Of what we knew, even then,
Were the skeletons of
Some glorious leaf lost forest.

***

Naughty Pine and Norsky Wood

Knotty pine on the living room walls
I was 16, with a fever, at home
In a big arm chair
You were the longhaired girl
I dreamed
There were cracks in the ceiling
I dreamed you through
To the tune on the Motorola
"I once had a girl, or should I say
She once had me?"*
You were my Norsky Blond on Blond*

I woke up wet, sweat and desire,
A happy ending happened along
So many years later, and here you are:
You lit the fire,
"Isn't if good, Norwegian wood?"*4

***

Stone Cold Winding Sheets

She took him in with a manic spin,
A twist of lust in
A cocktail squeeze—
She dressed him down
With hysterical style,
Like a haberdasher
Wit needles for eyes—

And now all that's left is whole cloth and souls—
He's wrapped all in hole cloth, coffin, concrete,
Out on the hillside, stone cold in winding sheets

***

Three Muses: Pheasant Lounge (1962)

Two sit enthroned,
Big backs backed to the
Hardwood earth grained
Horseshoe bar

---

4 Lennon/McCartney; Bob Dylan

One: Bouffant and budding,
Soon too bountiful,
Too thick in waist and arms,
Rounded purse lipped
Pig nosed, pink rose
Bound to pounds too soon

The other one,
Skinny as an REA pole,
Slinky as barbed wire spirals,
With red lips like
Blood plums,
And make up enough
For white face or
Whitsunday pancakes
With sausage on the side

Telecaster sounds of Telstar twang,
Reverse the lust, my vision—
12 years old, I peek in the door,
Telescoped down decades
As the six string zing of satellite
Dreamers tantalizes juke rock
Box—jammed between my ears:
Neon Pheasant, all red, white and blue

One muse all legs, arms and long gaits,
Straight haired in bangs,
Her limbs lasso tight with
The tension of braided rope
The corded muscles
She's not with the other girls, red faced
She's dark eye browed and blue eyed, too,
Wild as a mare at the end of a rope,
Just before the tension,

The taut-side step leap, Annie!

Cowboys and farmers look out!!!
Two muses will lead you to graves.

Too strung out, I'm twanging,
Sprung twine like a bowstring

Look in the shadows
Past the juke box lights,
The august of Augusts,
The curve of the bar and brass rail

Here in the shadows of southern comfort,
Some kind of old fashioned,
There's the third muse
Just turned out and still at 21

She waits for the Beatles,
The back beat in rhythm,
The rock in the roll of the floor

This young muse sighs
The song's 3/4 time
She drinks up and
Slowly slides out,
And (somehow its 1966;
Then its 1993),
Around the tables
And the white foreheads,
The tempted, sunburned hands,
She wanders in search
Of the big beat outside
Past the creak of the swinging door
Her hair to her shoulders,

She will soon learn the name
For her yearning,
Learn to call it the blues

By next year, this time, she'll be in New York,
And never come home until she buys the ranch.

***

Restaurant up the Road on A Western Friday

Had seats in the booths that were
Printed with patterns of Navaho blankets.
My mother gave me a pencil and paper
I drew and pretended:
Yellow for stars,
Green for the earth,
Red for fire
And blue for sky and water.
Even then I knew sky and water
Was the same thing,
Just observed from two directions.
I knew up from down.
There were no chardonnays
Or white zinfandels in
This reservation town.
Beer was not served
Unless you walked over
Into the bar
On the gun smoke side
Of the swinging doors.
Two happy fat girls
Sat at the next table over,
Their Colas raised in a toast.
All of these things were real,

Didn't know they were metaphors:
To the girls in the reservation town
In the booth, a town or so south from me,
Where there is the casino now,
And buffet with prime rib,
And maybe an oil well for
The new tribal council.
To those girls I cry:
Drink up, chubby beauties; drink up!

***

All the way from Fargo to Billings,
With no more stops on the line,
In the town called the "White City"
The rails are gone.
The mounds are left, weed covered useless dikes
To protect the white city on
The north and south sides, protect us
From success, from a future, from BOOM or BUST.

Christ himself rides the frozen
Rails with a cougar in the night.
The monks at the Abbey in
Richardton hear him call from
Their simple beds.
The twin towers of the Abbey
Call back to Christ and cougar.

Just south of there on the white ground,
The white city, The Spot sleeps on,
But friends on the farm
Just south of the place the meteor
Hit many years ago are awake:
"Why wouldn't it hit here?

(We kids said) Nothing
Ever lands around here."

In the morning after
The freight flew through
With the lonely lights of
Cars on I-94
(North of white City of course),
Our friend goes out to
Feed the cows at 12 below
And sees cougar tracks,
"Not bobcat or lynx",
Tracks running east to west,
Past the chicken coop
(You still have chickens?)
And the cattle shed,
Through the shelter belt
(Still have shelterbelts?
Yes and only three years old,
On the outside, pine, this time),
On out to the coulee and the butte beyond.

TS Eliot got it wrong for the White City breaks.
It wasn't Christ the tiger.
It was Christ the Cougar in America,
Rolling across the plains
At 70 miles an hour,
Not even side-lined for the coal train east,
And you heard him in your holy
Orders of sleep.

He came with the whine of car
Tires on the summer night highway,
The rumble of thunder and harvest
From the old grain trucks,

At the long blast of the whistle
From long frozen pasts,
Rolling from Round Head Fargo
To cowboy Coal Strip
(what a name for a coal town),
And then to the mountains beyond.

***

I dream I am playing
"Gloria" on my misty old Gibson Guitar,
Long dead with my foot through its middle.
She pokes me: "What are you doing?"
Awake, I shrug,
"I dreamed I was playing my dead guitar."
She rolls over and tosses her hair on the pillow.
"I thought you were having a fit."
"I was; (I AM) I was"

I felt like Ray Charles in "Walk The Line".
Wasn't that Johnny Cash?
Which do I mean?
Hopefully both.
Didn't they both wear black?

{Sunset, Sunday afternoon again,
That dusty time of the yearning
For God and a Bloody Mary—
A flock of gulls or terns,
Huge, white as a bird can be,
Circled, almost collided,
Swooped down on something
In a shadowed,
Freshly (I wrote fleshly first time around, in pencil.
Truth comes in mis-aligned lead lines of meaning.)

Harvested stubbly field—not one
Large body of water for miles around,
No digital cameras either,
But I knew we were being observed
Right there on the living room couch,
With some kind of gentle compassion.}

My love, I have no keys to open the
Mysterious doors of creation,
So I lay my fingers on the frets and play
On a perfectly square white piece of paper,
In writing even worse than my own:
Each moment is a story.
Every story is a poem.
And the poem is memory.
So memory is story,
And moments are made up, by God!
I tell, therefore I YAM, I am—Sam!
(Descartes, Popeye the Sailor, Dr. Seuss)>

***

The pop of a 12 gauge in the
Russian olives north of the house
Or the cracking of deer rifles
Later that fall—

{The Oriental Prince Cock of The Spot,
Pre-Raphaelite Pheasant—
Or the buck all crowned, golden brown
As he leaps fences and roads,
Bullet proofed in my words}

I don't care for these sounds.
I am like the little boy who hates

The pop of exploding balloons
In the mornings and evenings
Of summers and winters.
John, next door in the coulee,
Feeds the old cock
Who scrapes away with his
Cockney fiddle crow (as in bow
A Celtic cock, you see?).

The pop and crack
Of the same Russian olive
Cut and dried in our woodstove
Makes the sounds of comfort and joy.

But the air of that town where I grew up
Was so full of love and dreams
That I was able to gallop around
In great Prussian leaps beneath the sky,
In 4/4 time, a march-like rock and roll.
I never took time for moments,
And was always lost in the moment,
Missing the legal time; Oh! Clocks!
Even in second grade:
STOP DAYDREAMING RICKY!!!!
Relativity—connection—
Mrs. Egress with the sticky red lips—
Who needed video memory then?

I see you all,
My beloved and hated beautiful friends.
We moved, you moved in the holy seasons
(Suspended between four seasons, Christmas,
Easter, summer, and the
Endless decent through October to Halloween).
It was as if we went sled riding on our bikes

In sun burned snow on freezing hot days
Of Jack O Lantern, evergreen, red light—
Easter egg, fireworks resurrection birth: all one.
This is a spot where I should sigh out loud,
There on the wide streets of the valley,
Caught between the Lutheran fieldstone fortress
And the bricks walls of St. Vincent church,
With the courthouse on one side
And the water tower high on the other hill.
We made a feast of seasons out of one valley town,
Sandwiched between Water, Word, Bread and Wine (D)
With the Law to the Far East of us all.

"Zip code is a surrogate for economic status."
Richard H. Hersh, Ed D (10/24/07)

In my small town you can say this to
The folks passing by, and they may
Look at you askance and smile
They might even speak to you: "58646"

Tell it to the folks down in the 9th Ward today
In New Orleans
The zip code holds steady
When the whole damn
Postal service is washed away

Or the folks in the San Diego
Firestorm: last week—
Hunkered down like
Marines under fire
In their own stadium
With Starbucks and John Travolta:
"Deliveries may be held up"

Water and fire,
Poor black or western dreamer,
Each their disasters,
Fire, water, earth and air=soul

There is an elemental science to zip codes
That only nature herself can change

"Come home up the hill in the last light",
Means that pretty soon
You turn the corner,
Look up at the wide empty windows
Where the light strikes the tint
"No one inside," the windows say
Then you will feel more alone
Than if you were standing by
Yourself 10 miles west of town

I get angry defending my town
I have to remember it all,
But black words leave my mouth
Out come my black angers,
Dark sarcastic suggestions to the world
Outside my zip code and mind
Commands issue from my lips
(As if I know answers)
My tongue should be a stiff
Stump by now,
Or a pile of ashes to choke my throat
It all comes from the fact that
I am trying to show you our beauty
But I open my mouth
Instead of strawberries or tulips,
Cucumbers or pink rose bush blossoms,
Out come these words!

Women duck, lower their heads,
Think less of my peasant mouth
Men get edgy and clench their teeth
I make little children afraid.
Back to Christmas
In a green arm chair,
Beside a wood stove named 'Yodel',
A Norsky model, you know,
On my left,
And the big wide windows
To keep me feeling out in the open
The nearly Solstice light
Warms the ponds of glass

When I close my eyes
The right eye sees that wild rose pink
Which slowly turns tulip purple blue
Near the bridge of my nose
The left eye sees a woolly black,
Like the ether sleep when my tonsils went

I hear the wind chimes
Out front of my friend's house down the street,
Now, as distant harness bells,
The bells left in the barn when you died,
And my father and I ran the cattle
The last year before
My aunts and uncles sold the land
In the madness of 5 buck a bushel wheat

I keep my eyes shut
I am here to remember
The pasts of these Christmas ghosts

***

Sleep talking that night,
At the edge of 10 and the end of 9,
He sits up in his nest of a bed,
Looks at me with wide sleeping eyes
And says, "Up early; it's a game," or
"It's a game; how high you climb"
Then, he speaks these words clearly.
 I remember, for sure:
"It's like a religion, or a myth"
He lies down, rolls over and sleeps.

In this space between 9 and 10
His sleep talk says more than
The Arhats, Bodhisattvas'
Law giving shepherds, Son of Men or
Wife-stealing, harp-playing Kings

***

I have known for years that
My father the WWII veteran knows some things.
He stared down the clocks,
Takes care of his sisters,
Won't shrink at blood,
"bounced bullets off my eye balls
And caught mortar shells in my teeth,"
And has a way to find things to do each day

He found his dead buddy Arnold
Who was buried in Wall Nut Grove,
Somewhere in Western Minnesota.
The girl that worked at the Memorial there
Was impressed and wanted some tales.
He should have asked her for a date.

Ten years ago he would have made her blush.

He knows apples are good for horses, pigs and pies
The horses' snort for joy
The pigs grow intelligent and meaty
Apple pies will charm entire clans
He knows the pain and causes of the gout

When my son finds the dead rabbit on the
Gravel path on the east side of the house,
It does not bother the old man that it is raining
He gets a shovel, buries the murdered (teeth marks)
Rabbit with honors,
Right next to Saint Thomas, the Hermit Crab,
And finds the sensible healing words
Where did he learn these methods?
From his Frisian Grandma, and lone-ranger mother
16 miles south of the Spot That God Forgot

***

Thinking about Chinese poets who drink too much wine
On this windy day after a morning rain,
And a woman said the sky was "robin egg shell blue" (you,
    Jo),
And the wind is the wind I remember from
The Spot where I grew up and it blew
Deep with that blue and sunlight
Right down main-street one June morning,
Past the armory and swimming pool,
Kicked up Popsicle sticks and a bit of
Not so wet cottonwood fluff,
Past the Wolf Den and The Holiday House,
Picked up no wrappers because main street
Was that clean, even in front of

The Commercial Bank of Mott
With the giant clock in front,
And though the bank refused to flex
Its bricks against the wind
Or open the vault and give all
The money back to the flat-pursed people,
The wind did blow the ash off
Bobby the Banker's big cigar,
And the wind did assist
Bob the druggist
As he swept his sidewalk south
With the broom
In the direction of the bakery,
And the Jelly donuts called Bismarck
With the smell of hot ovens,
And past the Pheasant Lounge and Lunch,
All the way past the post office door,
Mosher Ford garage and into the
Brown, honey-creamed, rushing Cannonball River.

***

That same wind blew here in the Magic City today,
And two gold glazed young deer,
A doe, and a buck with sprouts for horns,
Crossed the street
While the robins beat up the Grackles
On my front lawn,
And some kind of little lark
Blew a song like a morning gospel
Tune on a hand carved wooden trumpet,
And a man in boots and baggy pants,
With a walking stick and floppy
Hat, a beard to his chest,
Strolled by with the walk of

A long time walking job,
Looked at our house,
Stood still for the deer
Until they were done with
The green apples on the tree
By the yellow house,
Nodded his head and raised
His staff when he saw me in the
Sunroom window watching,
And headed south, down the hill
And into the bigger town

Now, the wind still blows
In both of the towns I love
Where are you my companion?
Remember this to make
The moment of reveal—u (nc) tion clear.

Out on the road
The tall folk singer
Cannot afford
To have a cold,
But she does,
Cannot afford
The High Plains
Creole Back up Band,
She has none—
3 days lost
In the same motel
With the cardboard
Impressions
On the walls,
The windmills
And empty farms,
The village that

Even Currier and Ives
Would not try to create.
The motel maids
In Winnipeg speak Spanish
Once she reluctantly
Crosses the border into North Dakota,
She finds that the 7UP
And the dried noodle soup
Packets from the C Store really help

She stands on stage in the Student Union
On the prairie that makes many poets and farmers despair,
A place named "The Beaver Dam",
She strums up an E 7th chord,
Smiles to the mike,
Yells, "I am from Chicago!"
The students from Zap, Golden Valley,
Gackle and Mott
Are so young they missed Johnny Carson's joke,
And they wait for folk music,
Still, with their I pod corks in their ears

The Praise Singer cannot know us well:

We who are stooped like burros
To the boom and bust of the Halliburton world;
Nature's nurse of song we need you
Sing over the dead trees that
Hang down on the abandoned shelterbelts,
So we don't axe them and burn them.
We burn the exoskeletons of the
Ancient living souls of the world
And wait for our doled out trickling "growth"
With drool on our dirty chins:
Idiot children of a merciful God,

We can't see or hear the wind blow

She sings, this singer:
Even the dogs in our town,
Even the barkers and ankle biters,
Wangsvick's golden collie,
And you, Fawnie,
Growling little Pekinese,
Mother of my dog Ringo!

These dogs all have souls
They weep for the little
Girl's shins as they bite
They weep and give thanks
For the ankles on bikes
The little girls pedal
Dogs love the hot July days—
Dogs love the Praise singer's song
She is one her way with
Wisdom in her strings, White City
The High Plains Creoles
Are coming along to play for free

Popsicles melt in a daze,
And the sticks do just that:
On fingers, on streets
Where sticks fall
From hot fingers,
A hot second lost
And an hour at least.
A Popsicle drips
As the little dogs yip
At your shins.
Your bicycle tires
Stick to the streets,

And the world smells
Of sunburn, hot tar
Cut grass and
Chlorine from the
Public pool

Pleasure was complex
In simple the place where I lived,
On either side of
The slamming screen doors,
A new pair of blue jeans,
Old Milwaukee and Schlitz
(there's the joke of the rhyming),
Sweat, work (avoided), mosquitoes,
Weeds in the garden,
Grackles, meadowlarks,
Orange robin choirs,
Mobs of sparrows in winter
By the empty grain bins,
Vodka, whiskey, schnapps
To save bodies from ice,
The breath from the millions
Of exhaling blades of grass
That aired from the roots
From under the snow and
Gave us fresh sky all winter.

And Susanne DeLaPointe:
Say it! A beautiful girl
And a name as great as a river,
Even in (1962?) when Kennedy won,
even that year,
And lust turned to love in living:
Susanne was faster, pretty,
And stronger than all the boys,

Never cried, and she was a Democrat too

And Democrats too—
My farmer Grandma taught
The art of liberation,
To love, to learn and love
(It takes two wings for
This republic to fly;
Eagle or turkey, it flies)
Farmers Union Grandma:
Strong lava soap,
Pigeons, chickens, geese
And ducks,
Her democrat's hand on the
On the bloody hatchet
The days we butchered the chickens,
Democratic flowers of
Feathers and blood on the
Sandy soil,
Chicken head's wide eyes,
(Eyes to see all)
In the Gospel of North Dakota

When Grandpa left
She sent him to hell,
Or Deadwood, South Dakota,
And turned her silent power
To love on her clan:
Grandchildren, neighbors' kids,
Old alcoholics, wandering dogs,
We lived in her republic of love
It was fierce, hard and true
Her eyes saw past us all

Let them stagger in the street.

At one point they are funny.
At some point they are dying.
Even the drunkards in
Our town are loved
With our true puppy love,
Love as tough as the seat of a leather saddle.
Hank was treated like the king
On the southern townships
Down at the Pheasant Lounge.
Uncle George stopped
The mayor one Friday night
In front of the Holiday House,
Our stern-wheeler hotel,
And we all cheered him on
As the Democratic mayor
Agreed to move the cars
Off the sidewalk,
So Uncle George,
A Bull elephant in Bib overalls,
Could stagger in peace,
Even though any Empirocist
Can see there are no cars
On the sidewalks at all.

Drunks in this town
Are our spiritual bells?
Veterans of wars and
Stock market, oil depressions,
Orphans run off the land
By bankers from Fargo on East,
Manny happy loss and
Shickcago grain traders too.
The Mayor, a failed farmer himself,
Helps us to understand.
The high school band

Plays a march at the
Intersection of Commercial bank,
Johnson's Jewelry,
The Holiday House
And the apartments on the
Northwest corner (the old bank?
Someone must remember.)
We love so much the past is a fog.

***

I don't believe in global warming he says,
Surrounded by the wide eyes of his fellow
High school classmates.
They take his words with equal parts
Wonder, fear and scorn.

I don't believe in world hunger either.
Not even when you see pictures on TV?
The skinny girl in the pitch dyed black hair,
Her face a white flag,
Thin lipped, blue white, bone-white angry
Gives the wise woman stare.

May be for a minute when I see the picture,
But then I forget it right away.
His pride at her fury makes him smile a bit.
She is pretty; he is noticed.
This is still a small town school;
Might as well be 1968

The mother and father
Load a pike boned, death camp candidate,
16 years old, into a van
And drive straight through,

On the edge of a blizzard,
Past thousands of kids
In hundreds of small towns
Dressed in white landscapes
To a clinic for her, 900 miles away.
She is so skinny, her gall bladder stopped
She cannot possibly eat,
Ashen, can't get dates,
And she is pretty too.
No one will be allowed to visit
Her translucent body
For at least 4 days.
One of her best friends is
Barely pregnant, period missed last week.

Billions too many,
Parts of America and
Whole regions of Africa
Dying of two kinds of hunger,
Billions too many
born every year.
Welcome to the global village.
How much more of this village will it take?

There is no snow out her window, then too much.
There is no food, or else there is always too much.
We created the curses of nature
And made our children the future's fools.
We are the one's who forced the locks in the land of plenty,
Busted the atom, pumped the oil from
Prairies, tundra and desert,
Engineered sexed up twigs shaped like girls,
The steroid boys in the third floor lock up,
The failed farmers out growing weed and cooking meth.

No excuses. Come on. Don't give lines about choices to
    chance.
Fat talk show conservative/liberal jack—
We threw the gods out of the cockpit,
Jumped in ourselves
And drove our combustible planet
To the limits of stone, water, earth, air and soul.

***

So Here's A Young Cowboy[5]

He rides a small scooter,
Along the old strip mall
The torn parking lot
He's skinny in tall hat,
Blue jeans and tall boots,
Where is he going
In Bonetown boom town?
Where is his pick up
And where is his horse?
Where is his rig
And where is his poke?
He came from the far south
To find easy money
He's riding a scooter
It's some kind of joke

***

Pheasant, Turkey, Crow and Squirrel

She's skinny and pretty, 18, a mother,

---

[5] To the tune of "Streets of Laredo"

Already stretched thin by air brush and dreams
Three months along with her second child
She widens her big eye and tells us this tale:

"I'm cursed; these animals, they do not like me!
When I had my first baby, the day I came home
I opened the window, in the bedroom upstairs
And a Pheasant flew in! Starts wrecking and flapping,
Crashing, I'm screaming—my Dad came running
And finally just killed it—it just wouldn't fly!

Then, not much later, just two months or three,
I get into my car, start up the engine and try
To back out of the driveway—there's grinding,
And dragging—I get out to look and
And a great big black turkey goes flapping and
Banging the street—I'm screaming,
My dad comes, and gets a scoop shovel
To poke the thing loose, and he breaks its neck,
So another wild bird in my life ends up dead!

I'm here on the campus, just last October,
In brand new sun glasses, a nice afternoon,
When, I swear, (I have witnesses; they helped me out)
This big crow starts diving right at my face
And knocks off my glasses—just then this
Tall guy starts swinging a racquet and chases
The crazy big crow away—my glasses!
God, but that crow was so huge!

Wait, I'm not done—just last week, I'm walking
Past Old Main, a squirrel jumps on my
Back off a dumpster and chases me, all the
Way to Harnett Hall, and two guys are
Yelling, chasing the squirrel, so I can just

Get in the door—I swear to God I'm so
Glad there aren't bears in this town"

Nature, like woman, comes into her own
In spite of community, family and laws,
Life feeds life and the rest we all should know

***

They Both Felt Left

He got in an argument with his own shadow
Neither could be moved to move all day
When the sun went down they both were lost

***

If I could not go to heaven but with a party, I would not go
there at all...
We have called by different names brethren of the same
principle. We are all Republicans, we are all Federalists. If
there be any among us who would wish to dissolve this union
or to change its republican form, let them stand undisturbed
as monument of the safety with which error of opinion may
be tolerated where reason is left free to combat it.

(Thomas Jefferson NYTBR 9/17/07)

This is the Holy Wisdom of Putt Putt Golf, Thomas,
Up there where you and Nixon,
And all the Black Hemmings kids,
And all the black burned Vietnamese babies
Are now aware of the lack of need for political parties.
Welcome to the White City.
You are 33 miles South of Assumption Abbey

Just south of Interstate 94.
Ask dead Ike, who used our defense
Against another political foe, Stalin and Khrushchev
(they are dead too),
To build these oil burning lanes of speed and joy.

Today you will be playing Putt Putt golf
With Brendon Iver Watson, then aged 9, now 10 and then
Here at the Pool Side Drive Inn
On a course perfected
And moved from the Magic City,
Here to the Spot God did not quite forget

Blue air, ah, breath it in,
Not the smoke of Virginia
Or the Capitol's pestilential air

There is a grass blowing Northwest wind on this hill
Cottonwood leaves flap like small green wings in the sun
The sound and sight of clear running water,
Piped from deep down below—
You won't even hear the hum the electrical pumps
The gravel is mosaic, abstract relief,
Laid out by clear running water
The course is all down hill from here,
6 colors of balls
That thunk to the swing of
The short little rubber headed clubs,
The smell of fries from the Pool Side grill
And the curved ellipsis of time—Einstein style,
Or EGO EIMI—let Jefferson's prairie grid be gone
The perfect putt, the impossible bounce,
Through gates, over wedges, embankments,
Through the fortifications of fancy,
A mad architect, maybe Holy Wisdom disguised in a beard,

Back when the White City was plated and mapped for now.
The 9th hole is a windmill with real, miniature cows at the
    tank;
Then the final hole, the down hill vortex, freedom in
The speed of a golf ball hit by a rubber-headed club,
Impossible to miss!

***

Swept As Clean As a Kitchen Floor

I keep deluding myself
I think I can find a new way
To show the sky tonight
By using these words again:
"Dark", "star", "wind"
Some kind of Shakespeare or Tolstoy,
Dakota baked, frozen,
Stratford born on the yellow grass
Cannonball river breaks
Wants to be lord of the manor,
Worshiped by the serfs he frees,
Robin Hood meets Trotsky
Out on the prophetic, violent plains:

I am here to read the signs in the sky,
Short grass, rocks, and all faces, like books
(The cat curls up, asleep on the shelves)
I am here to try and play this guitar
In the tone of wasp sting honey frost
Barbed wire slip fingered greased ice
On the power lines until my fingers
Can't shape a looping series of chords
And the parabolic progression ends

Senile and pants pissed I still will
Hum these high plains Creole gospel
Tunes until your lovely face
Is all that is left in my cleansed
An empty, ancient mind,
I'll be swept as clean as a
Kitchen floor on Saturday,
A gold and cold blue afternoon

***

Bed Room Prayers...

...Were said against the evil in the outside dark
When I was shy, so sweet, and so young—
The dog headed God of Egyptian myth,
Ala Cecil B. DeMille
(I prayed for Moses, Charlton Heston,
Armed with Staff, instead of
Waving an M-16 above his head)—

I feared Count Dracula himself and
Prayed to the cross above my bed,
That Jesus beacon glowing blue at night—
But now in winter when covers touch my nose,
The dark of 60 broken years of me wells up,
All from the sea-fish soul of sin inside—
This inside dark is real, here,
Unlike the dark outside that comes and goes—
My vision spots the devil, dark—
That devil looks like me—
What do I do? You know, you know,
Next to me in bed for all the years—
I pull your body close; my absolution comes—

The fact of love, just you my girl,
Resurrects the sweetest bedtime prayer.

***

The Bedroom Door

If you can live with the family, and they can live with you
The door to love is opened wide
Romeo and Juliet were lodestars, romantic lord, but they were
    fiction too
Even then, dagger and poison got them both
You do not sleep with the family of the lover who rules your
    soul,
But if you want to sleep in peace, make sure the family is in
    the house
Then lock and bar the bedroom door—love breaks
The star-crossed cage and flies again

***

Kitchen Help

I am still a minstrel
I have seen mistrials
I wish I were a mistral

You want me to work at the kitchen sink, I will
But then when the grease soaped dishes melt
And the cats dip their whiskers into your scraps
While the puppy dogs lick my scrapes
Will you allow me to strum my guitar
On the drum of your heart?
Will you ears play your feet to the beat while I sing?

***

Accidental Connection for the Day

"I got a call from my broker/my broker told me I was
      broke"—Paul Simon

The Untied States of America are broke, or nearly, on the
      edge
the Donkeys and Elephants agree.

"One thing is for certain/life is great at Halliburton"—Mick
      Jagger and Keith Richards

Oil seems to be doing well, if not the people impacted by the
      oil,
In North Dakota or in the Mid East.

The death rate among American troops is higher in the
      Middle East than at
any time since the war in Afghanistan began.

A Russian student of mine said, "If you should never get in a
      ground war in Europe,

Stop. Multiply the cost by 1000, and you will see the result of
      getting in a ground
war in Afghanistan."

Who needs prophets or pundits? We have Rock and Roll.

***

Dance Floor Your Mind

Microsoft Outlook Voice Mail Preview
From my wife: "(confidence is low)"—

"Hi phones can and dance floor your mind."

Created by Microsoft Technology,
My love, my life-long one,
You seem to call me out to two-step
Via the ghosts in the machine:
"Dance floor your mind," Amen

***

Spoken As a True Poet
(Found poem, DW Fuller)

"My iPad
Is a virtual,
Predicative nominative
Blunder that
Causes most
Of its users
To
Wander around with their heads misplaced,
Staring into their hand with total disregard
To the roses and the birds," He said

***

The Rest of the Day

The sunrise aligns with the valley
In a way that's just right
So the first light brushes
The tops of the bare oaks
Below with the kind of color

A photographer or painter
Would just wait to produce
Now it's all overcast, looks like snow
Could still set in by noon
I want to paint that light I saw
On the tree tops, blend
Shades and brush to remember
That lights the rest of the day

My sense of beginning is in
The ending which I do not understand
And afternoon is blue and long
And I sleep when I can
Until the night gets on
And then I can't sleep and so
Sense of rising and falling
Action is more like the ocean,
Less like Aristotle's
Extremely nasty arc
I rewrite my masterpiece
Until the Master and Mistress
Come home to end part 2
And then who knows how the
The tale comes out of this ass?

In my town we tell the stories
Over until they make their own endings
Or until they get in the Bible
So I digress that this may end
Or begin as the Water Tower
Glows in the late dusk,
A one car rolls down our
Mainstreet as wide as a river
And the door of the Pheasant
Lounge opens wide to my face

Let your Cracke Pot Minstrel
Hang around in peace
Until the strings are unstrung
And restrung and tunes
On the strands of God's
Own comic Cosmic DNA

About the Author:

For Immediate and Repeated Release

On April 1st, the Spencer Bradahl Memorial Library will hostess a new sound from a group that is older than you would think. The High Plains Creoles, Formerly the Doctors, formerly the Wheat Kings, right after they were the High Plains Creoles are, for the moment, a cosmic string band made up of Dr Eric Anderson (cello and snarling smirks), Dr Ron Fischer (Bass guitar and Torah), Dr. Selmer Moen (mandolin, pipe organ, accordion, piano, dobro, and steel that guitar, as well as computers), and the Reluctant Reverend, Master of Divinity, ND associate Poet Larryette, and preacher of constant reformation, especially his own (guitar, vocables, left leaning loosely learned leaping elliptical lyrics) and the biggest ego of the band, a crack pot propheteer himself.

Rick watson.

They play reformation based Judeo Christian Creole Ghost Dance Shekinah music on demand, whether the weather or the demand is great or not, all kinds of songs that Watson, Mott's own former village idiot, wrote or makes up on the spot, most underehearsed (call it CHASS< CHUNIOR, if you know what's good fer ye), and many of which they hope to never play again. Citizens of dubious standing and background, including some with terminal degrees and illnesses, have found this enselmerbow to be delightening, entertaining, sexy, poetic, religious, politically promising, etc. They will play from their vast imagined catalogue of nearly unknown songs (even to them) at the library any time any of you show up.

There will be a keg, fried meat, greasy pastries and extremely tautand wildly strong coffee. Most recently the boys wowed in rural Border Central, up on the High Line in the nearly dead town of Driano by exorcising one huge vulture and a flock of Monarch butterflies from the tranced out body of MS Emilia Bach, church organist and local liberal Catholic baiter and hater.

All this information has been made available to us here at the Mott Homesteader Press by the well-know and deeply mistrusted agent, Gold Farb Beaver Booster, manager and laundry specialist, on parole from the Ward County Jail where he was nabbed confabbing with the jailor's spouse in flagrante delectation.

We at the Homesteader look forward to reviewing the show! What a boost for old Spencer's Memorial library and its collection of ancient and modern books running back to the days when the main street was wide and filled with suckers on Friday and Saturday GNights—Remember Borges, the blind librarian?!

www.ingramcontent.com/pod-product-compliance
Lightning Source LLC
Chambersburg PA
CBHW061820040426
42447CB00012B/2740